UNLOCKING STRATEGIC INNOVATION

This new book explores how firms achieve competitive advantage in a disruptive, digital and globalized business landscape.

An integrative framework, 'The Four Rs of Competitive Success', is introduced, which covers the four core pillars of global strategy: resources and capabilities, technology and innovation (recombination), internationalization and international markets (reach), and physical and virtual location (roots). It then explains how competitive advantage is achieved through an interaction of these four drivers against the backdrop of a globalized and digitized world. It is uniquely practical in its approach, combining theoretical understanding with international case studies and real-life examples throughout each chapter, including Apple, IKEA and Microsoft.

Unlocking Strategic Innovation is concise, applied reading for postgraduate students studying international business, corporate strategy, innovation and digital strategy, as well as academics in the field. It will also be important reading for practitioners looking to gain further understanding of how firms compete and flourish in a global and technology-driven environment.

Surja Datta is a senior lecturer in Strategy and Innovation at Oxford Brookes University, UK. Surja has published extensively, including books, book chapters and journal articles, and is Associate Editor of an international technology management journal. His research interests include business history, innovation and creativity.

Sandeep Roy is a growth innovation advisor with specialisms in business model innovation, disruptive growth and digital strategy. He has over 25 years of industry experience, working with renowned multinationals such as Lloyds Banking Group, Tata Consulting, Wipro, Citigroup, Standard Chartered Bank and American Express Bank.

Tobias Kutzewski is currently conducting research towards his PhD at VU University, Amsterdam, the Netherlands. His research interests include entrepreneurship, innovation and research methods. Furthermore, Tobias works as an interim finance manager and is a chartered accountant at the ACCA. He gained extensive practice experience working with Accenture, Deloitte, ING and at a Venture Capital Fund.

UNLOCKING STRATEGIC INNOVATION

Competitive Success in a Disruptive Environment

Surja Datta, Sandeep Roy and Tobias Kutzewski

Routledge
Taylor & Francis Group

LONDON AND NEW YORK

First published 2021
by Routledge
2 Park Square, Milton Park, Abingdon, Oxon OX14 4RN

and by Routledge
52 Vanderbilt Avenue, New York, NY 10017

Routledge is an imprint of the Taylor & Francis Group, an informa business

British Library Cataloguing-in-Publication Data
A catalogue record for this book is available from the British Library

Library of Congress Cataloging-in-Publication Data
Names: Datta, Surja, author. | Roy, Sandeep, 1965– author. |
Kutzewski, Tobias, 1980– author.
Title: Unlocking strategic innovation: competitive success in a disruptive
environment / Surja Datta, Sandeep Roy and Tobias Kutzewski.
Description: New York: Routledge, 2021. |
Includes bibliographical references and index.
Identifiers: LCCN 2020044237 (print) |
LCCN 2020044238 (ebook) | ISBN 9780367322496 (hardback) |
ISBN 9780367322502 (paperback) | ISBN 9780429317514 (ebook)
Subjects: LCSH: Competition. | Business enterprises–Technological
innovations. | Business enterprises–International cooperation. |
Strategic planning. | Globalization–Economic aspects.
Classification: LCC HD41 .D378 2021 (print) |
LCC HD41 (ebook) | DDC 658.4/063–dc23
LC record available at https://lccn.loc.gov/2020044237
LC ebook record available at https://lccn.loc.gov/2020044238

ISBN: 978-0-367-32249-6 (hbk)
ISBN: 978-0-367-32250-2 (pbk)
ISBN: 978-0-429-31751-4 (ebk)

Typeset in Bembo
by Newgen Publishing UK

CONTENTS

FIGURES AND TABLE

Figures

Table

ACKNOWLEDGEMENTS

An academic book of this kind is inevitably a collaborative effort. You collaborate with your co-authors, but you also engage in intense mental dialogues with other scholars whose ideas have informed and enriched the contents of this volume. Moreover, we have been promiscuous and not limited ourselves to surveying the conventional strategic management field in our search for interesting insights. We have ventured into hitherto neglected domains like economic geography, social networks, optionality and evolutionary anthropology, and benefited enormously from these excursions. To all the scholars and thinkers whose insights have enriched this book, we express our gratitude.

A big thank you goes to Sophia Levine and Emmie Shand from Routledge. Without their encouragement and gentle prodding, this book would not have seen the light of the day.

The idea of the book germinated in an MBA classroom. Surja leads the core MBA module 'Global Strategy and Innovation' in Oxford Brookes University, and both the structure and content of the book have been shaped by the experience he accrued delivering it over several years. He would like to extend his thanks to past student cohorts of the module. The interactions that he has had with them have enriched this book in innumerable ways.

After a long stint in the industry, Tobias decided to pursue a PhD at VU University in Amsterdam, the Netherlands. Tobias would like to thank his colleagues and students at VU University for their valuable support.

At the end, we would like to thank our families. They have been our anchor. Surja would like to thank his wife Boni who (as usual) created the space for him to finish the project and his son Jishnu who did his duty and supplied the light entertainment. Sandeep would like to acknowledge his father who encouraged him to think big and his mother who showed him the path to lifelong learning because she did not have the opportunity to pursue higher education. Tobias is particularly grateful to his wife Henrike for her ongoing support in his academic work and to Jakob, Kolja and Alma for providing unmeasurable joy to this journey of learning.

1

INTRODUCTION

In 1902, the Minnesota Mining and Manufacturing Company was established with the intention to extract corundum, an aluminium oxide. In the same year, a new speed record was set in France by Léon Serpollet; driving a car with a steam-engine. Over more than one century, the number of changes the company experienced are countless – two World Wars occurred, numerous political, social and economic changes as well as technological innovation affected the company. But not the company's prosperity. 3M, as the company is currently known, is one of the most innovative and adaptive companies in the world. So, how has 3M achieved this considerable feat?

This book is concerned with one main question. How do firms achieve competitive advantage within an increasingly disruptive environment? The disruption comes in various forms. Your products become obsolete, your services are no longer required, the business model of your firm is not fit for purpose, your competitors are suddenly not local but global. The disruptions and the consequent uncertainty are driven by two key factors – globalization and digitization. The current strategic thinking acknowledges that the process of globalization has gathered pace in the last thirty odd years, but it is strangely reluctant to accept that the complexity of the macro environment has therefore gone up exponentially. This book charts out a different course. It holds the view that driven by globalization and digitization, the business environment has altered paradigmatically. The changes are not incremental; they are radical. To thrive in this altered state, firms need an approach that is different from the one that delivered success in the second half of the twentieth century. Much of the current thinking on business strategy and innovation was developed in an era that was more stable, where the variables required to be considered for decision-making were relatively few. There is a need to adapt that thinking to the current reality, and this is one of the main goals of the book.

The ideas and the arguments of the book may appear relevant to only for-profit firms, but we hold the view that these are as relevant to not-for-profit enterprises, particularly those that compete in private markets. For example, Oxfam is a not-for-profit enterprise, but it is also a multinational firm competing with other for-profit organizations in multiple product markets. The theories, ideas and arguments presented in this book are valid for not-for-profit enterprises like Oxfam as well.

Much of the strategic management literature is preoccupied with the dynamics of large corporations, whereas the vast majority of business firms out there comprises small and medium sized enterprises (SMEs). There is then a disconnect between the theoretical ideas and the practice of strategy. This book attempts to redress this imbalance. We want this book to be useful to both students and practitioners of strategy. The theories, concepts and business cases that are covered in the book have been selected from the perspective of a representative business firm, and the representative firm is not the big multibillion pound generating corporation. Rather, it is an SME operating in a hypercompetitive market which is imbued with disruptive uncertainty.

When we say we are concerned with the competitive advantage of firms it may appear that we are essentially talking about firm level dynamics, like the fluctuations in available resources and changes in competences, as well as the business strategies of organizations to cope with those dynamic changes. However, this is not the case at all. It provides just the steppingstone to a much broader understanding of how companies are affected in their way of organizing. As we shall see in the following chapters, the competitive advantage of a firm is based on several key variables, firm-specific resources and competences being just one of them. The reality is that competitive success emerges out of a constellation of factors, some within the control of the firm, some outside of it. And yes, this means that chance plays a relevant role in firms' competitive success; however, following a popular saying, we can say that fortune tends to favour the prepared firm. Successful firms are not merely artefacts of a series of accidents, neither are they the results of some tremendously effective hyper-planning strategy evoked.

A brief note on the writing style. We want to avoid 'academese',[1] the jargon-laden passive style of writing that academics often use to communicate with other academics. As mentioned before, we want this book to be read by both students and practitioners. They are our main readers, not other academics. With this in mind, we have kept the writing style conversational, and have not burdened the text with excessive references. We have provided extensive endnotes and bibliography at the end of each chapter that reflects the solid theoretical underpinnings of this book, so readers who are interested in following through with any idea, theory or concept, can do so without any problem.

This book has a point of view. It does not merely consolidate the extant literature on competitive success, although our point of view is built on a synthesis of that body of knowledge. The main argument is that competitive success is delivered through the four Rs: Resources, Reach, Recombination and Roots. Each of these is discussed in detail in subsequent chapters, but briefly here: 'Resources' are those tangible and intangible assets that firms have access to and/or have control of. 'Reach' relates to the extent of the firm's operation. A multinational corporation (MNC) for example and for obvious reasons has more reach than a domestic firm. 'Recombination' is now widely recognized as the main process that brings about innovation: new products and services that provide the dynamism of the global economy. Last, but definitely not the least, is the matter of 'roots', the place from where the firm originates and/or is based. Place is often underappreciated as a factor of competitive success; we try to redress this imbalance in the book.

The four variables link with each other in interesting ways. For example, the 'roots' of an organization impact its 'reach' and 'resources' in a significant manner. We discuss the interdependencies between the four Rs in Chapter 8. There are of course other factors that merit consideration, but we hold that the four Rs are central to achieving competitive advantage; they matter even more in the current 'Age of Uncertainty'. This way of thinking also pushes back against prevalent mono-causal explanations of competitive success.

The four Rs act as prompters for evaluating firm competitiveness:

- Where are their roots?
- How far is their reach?
- What resources can they control and/or have access to?
- How good are they in recombining ideas and resources?

As we start answering these questions, an overall picture of a firm's competitive position starts to emerge. The four Rs framework (see Figure 1.1) is the meta concept of this book which helps us to integrate the insights generated in the individual chapters that follow. We hope that the interlinkages that exist between the four Rs would become apparent as you go through the chapters; however, we make them more explicit in the concluding chapter of the book.

The book is structured in the following way. In Chapter 2 (Globalization, digitization and disruptive uncertainty), we explain how the business environment has been transformed over the last thirty years and is now filled with high levels of uncertainty and disruption. We use the concept of Global Flows to demonstrate how these flows are making the external environment more disruptive. The speed

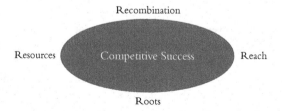

FIGURE 1.1 The four Rs of competitive success

of Global Flows has accelerated through digitization of business processes. We suggest in the chapter that focusing on the velocity of Global Flows, impacted by national 'barriers' and 'expeditors', is essential for developing an understanding of this disruptive uncertainty. We point out that this uncertainty is, however, Janus-faced – while it is true that firms can suffer losses from the disruption, they can also benefit from it. It is the latter which is often overlooked in business strategy texts. In this chapter, we elaborate on this duality of uncertainty.

Chapter 3 (Resources: Assets, capabilities and strategic positioning) explores the notions of resources and capabilities, and how they relate to competitive success. Firm-specific resources and capabilities are held to be central to the generation of competitive advantage in strategy texts. But how does one determine which resources and capabilities are key to competitive success? How do firms ensure that their resources deliver success within a changing environment? The chapter answers these key questions. An alternative perspective in strategic management is that profitable companies emerge out of attractive industries. The argument here is that the structure of the industry is the main driver of firm profitability. Strategic positioning of the firm is about achieving the 'fit' between organizational assets and industry dynamics. Both perspectives have their individual strengths and weaknesses and the chapter covers them in detail.

Chapter 4 (Recombination: The process of innovation) focuses on the relationship between innovation and the generation of competitive advantage. Innovation is essentially the process of creating something novel through the recombination of ideas, resources and capabilities. How does this recombination occur in practice? How critical is innovation for firm profitability? What kinds of innovation do firms specialize in? The chapter addresses these questions and explains how the disruptive environment is forcing firms to find new routes to innovation, Open Innovation being the most prominent among them.

There are very few sheltered industries out there that are immune to global competition. Chapter 5 (Reach: Going global) explores the link between international operations and competitive advantage. What benefits are accrued by extending one's reach? What are the barriers to extending reach? What additional organizational complexities arise when a firm goes global? What strategies do firms deploy to achieve competitive success in global markets? Why and how are some firms 'born global'? Is it even possible to achieve competitive success as a pure domestic player in today's disruptive environment? These questions are explored in detail in the chapter.

Chapter 6 (Roots: Power of the place) investigates a paradox. We live in the Age of Digitization; however, quite paradoxically, the firm's physical location has never been more critical to competitive success. It is not a coincidence that many successful 'digital' firms are clustered together in close physical proximity in the Silicon Valley. We are writing this book in the midst of the Covid-19 pandemic and efforts are ongoing across the globe to come up with efficient testing and of course a vaccine for immunization. These efforts are not equally distributed across the world, rather they are concentrated in specific places and Oxford is one of them. The bioscience cluster in Oxford has already produced a fast 90-minute test for Covid-19 and it is widely expected that the vaccine currently in development by Oxford University can deliver the desired outcome. It is very likely that this bioscience cluster in Oxford will get bigger going forward, as more pharmaceutical and biotech companies relocate to the region to benefit from the specialized knowledge that exists there. Place is underestimated as a success factor in conventional strategy textbooks. In contrast, we argue that place is one of the key determinants of firm competitiveness. Companies often have a choice of locations where they can put down roots, where they base their headquarters. That decision can enormously affect the competitive success of the firm in times to come. We explain the importance of roots or location in this chapter.

Chapter 7 (Creating options: Harnessing the power of uncertainty) juxtaposes the hyperrationality that underpins most strategy and innovation frameworks with the emerging idea of Optionality, which is essentially about embracing uncertainty. Optionality is about minimizing the downside while keeping the upside open. This requires a different mind-set when it comes to strategizing about competitive success. Optionality requires the organization to be comfortable with a series of small losses as that opens up the possibility of a big payoff. Conventional strategic thinking assumes that managers/strategists have perfect foresight which is obviously at odds with the reality. Option thinking does not demand such a superhuman feat from its practitioners; it requires them to be rational yet cognizant of the limits of that rationality. The chapter shows how some of the limitations of the conventional strategy frameworks can be overcome through insights generated from option thinking.

In conclusion, in Chapter 8 (Bringing it all together), we show how the integrative four Rs framework pulls together the four drivers of firm competitiveness. The linkages are illustrated through various case studies. It has been said that all theoretical ideas are products of their time. Our time is fraught with uncertainty and disruptions brought on by the twin forces of globalization and digitization. The endeavour here is put forward a framework that explains firm competitiveness in this dynamic environment.

A note on the case studies

We have provided several case illustrations in the following chapters. The cases have been carefully selected to complement the theories that have been discussed within the main text. Within the main text, we have referred to many business cases to illustrate the conceptual points that are being made. The long case studies within the boxes do not refer to the theories directly but they relate, one way or the other, to the theories covered in the chapter. These long case studies are designed to provoke conversations among students and practitioners about how they relate to the conceptual ideas discussed in the main sections. We have provided some kickstarter questions at the end of each case study; we call them 'pointers to strategic conversations'.

Note

1 See for example, Steven Pinker's engaging article on the topic 'Why Academics Stink at Writing' available at: https://stevenpinker.com/files/pinker/files/why_academics_stink_at_writing.pdf.

2

GLOBALIZATION, DIGITIZATION AND DISRUPTIVE UNCERTAINTY

Uncertainty and strategy are integrally linked together. Strategy is essentially about navigating an uncertain future. Yet, standard strategy texts treat uncertainty as a topic not worth exploring in detail. The macro environment is 'analysed' in a perfunctory manner using simplistic tools like the PEST (or its extension, the PESTLE) framework. These frameworks are underpinned by the assumption that it is possible for managers to logically identify the most relevant political, economic, social and technological factors in the environment that impact their organizations and take strategic actions accordingly. While this may (or may not) have worked in a more stable environment, we argue that this approach is problematic within the current context. Uncertainty is anathema to people who like to plan. Therefore, it is not surprising that conventional strategy thinking does not have much time for uncertainty; the planning paradigm[1] dominates traditional strategic management. Let us be clear, we are not suggesting that planning is unimportant. To be rational is to plan. What we do caution against is hyper-planning, which we discuss in more detail in Chapter 7 (Creating options: Harnessing the power of uncertainty).

The environment has become increasingly disruptive and uncertain due to the twin forces of globalization and digitization. The process of globalization, of course, has been happening for a very long time. But what is different now compared to the past is the pace of change. The other force, digitization, is, in comparison, of recent origin. It was ushered in with the invention of the internet and the World Wide Web, and explosive growth in communication technologies.

Global flows, barriers and expeditors

The *New York Times* columnist, Thomas Friedman, in his book *The World is Flat* (2006), suggested that the history of globalization can be classified into three epochs. For Friedman, Globalization 1.0, which he rather arbitrarily demarked as starting in

1490 and ending in 1820, was about countries. This was the era of colonization, the Age of Empires. International trade and investment happened mainly intra-Empire; for example the British set up the railways in India to run the colony. As Friedman puts it, the 'dynamic agent of globalisation in this era was the country. You went global through your country'.[2] In contrast, the chief actor in Globalization 2.0 (1820–2000) was the corporation. Multinationals such as IBM and Toyota were at the helm in this period. Globalization 3.0, the current era, Friedman concluded, is about individuals, who with their desktops or tablets, aided by the internet and World Wide Web, are now ready to conquer the globe.

Friedman's potted history of globalization is intuitive but largely inaccurate. For one thing, globalization did not start in the late fifteenth century. The history of globalization is as old as the history of humankind. Migration of people from one region to another is one of the many types of Global Flows[3] that are possible. When ancient humans migrated great distances by foot or boat, they not only colonized new geographical spaces; they also brought new ideas to places already occupied by other people. Even international trade has a very long history. Trade in goods was happening between cities in the Indus Valley civilization and Mesopotamia around 2000 BCE.[4] Perhaps where Friedman's classification is most wrong is in the claim that corporations have diminished in significance in the current era and individuals have taken up their place. The inaccuracy in the claim is increasingly obvious with the benefit of hindsight. The years since publication of Friedman's book have confirmed that the influence of big corporations has increased in the twenty-first century and not diminished. The early years of the current century have seen the emergence of technological giants such as Amazon, Facebook and Twitter. Their dominating presence in many aspects of our lives is now of great concern to activists and policymakers. We now have trillion-dollar companies (in terms of their market capitalization) like Apple, Amazon and Microsoft.[5] The virtual public space where we meet and communicate with each other is privately owned by giant social media companies and these organizations can and often do shut out specific individuals from the digital public square.[6]

Before Friedman, hyperglobalists like Kenichi Ohmae proclaimed the death of the nation-state (Ohmae, 1989). For hyperglobalists who were particularly vocal during the last two decades of the twentieth century, the nation-state is no longer the main actor in the Great Globalization Game – the multinational corporation is. So, we see that there is this particular way of thinking about the progress of globalization: the dominance of nation-state had given way to that of MNC in the last twenty-five years of the twentieth century, and now in the twenty-first century, to that of individuals. In this book, we argue that this way of thinking about globalization is mainly erroneous. Rather than speculating which actor was/is 'dominant' in which epoch, a more fruitful approach to understanding globalization is in focusing on how the roles of the leading players – such as nation-states, non-state actors including corporations and non-governmental organizations (NGOs), and multilateral agencies – have evolved in different eras.

The nation-state was, is and will remain (in the foreseeable future) one of the main actors of globalization, but its role has evolved. The way it impacted global trade in the eighteenth and nineteenth centuries is dramatically different from the way it now does. An analogy could be made here with the impact of parents on the lives of their children. The importance of parents has not diminished but parenting has evolved over the years. **Global Flows**, which we discuss below, is a framework that can be used to understand and analyse the roles of different key actors in the globalization process.

Globalization is one of the two meta processes that are creating the disruptive uncertainty. Sociologists like George Ritzer have characterized the situation as being 'liquid-like', where the old certainties melt away and things become a whole lot more uncertain. While a lot has been written on globalization, its role in creating disruptive uncertainty for corporations is not well understood. We explain how this uncertainty comes about through our Global Flows framework.

So, what are Global Flows? Simply put, they are movements in goods, services, capital, ideas and people across national boundaries. There are institutional structures that either act as barriers to or expeditors of Global Flows. Multilateral agencies like the World Trade Organization (WTO), World Bank and International Monetary Fund (IMF) are post-Second World War institutions that have expedited greatly Global Flows in goods, services and capital. Competitive success often depends on how expertly you can navigate these Global Flows. Multinational corporations have evolved to navigate Global Flows more efficiently than other organizational forms[7].

Two attributes of Global Flows are important to pinpoint:

a. At an abstract level, Global Flows can flow evenly across the globe. In the real world, the flows of goods, services, capital and people are extremely uneven. This is because of the presence of national level barriers and expeditors which are unevenly distributed across the geographical space. So, Global Flows are potentially global, but rarely so in practice.
b. Somewhat paradoxically, Global Flows are integrally connected with the idea of a nation-state. Just like international law, which would not exist without the presence of nation-states, Global Flows occur because they transcend national boundaries. There were flows of people, goods and services across vast geographical distances before the invention of nation-states, but in our schema, they were just 'movements' as there was, at the time, neither a conception of 'global' nor any notion of 'national'. The key point to note is this: even in today's globalized word, everything flows through the nation-state. Multilateral agencies, like the UN, WTO, IMF and World Bank, are propped up by nation-states; multilateral agencies literally cease to exist without their members who are exclusively made up of nation-states. The proliferation of the multilateral agencies in the post-Second World War era can give the impression that nation-states have faded into the background. Nothing can be further from the truth, as we explain below.

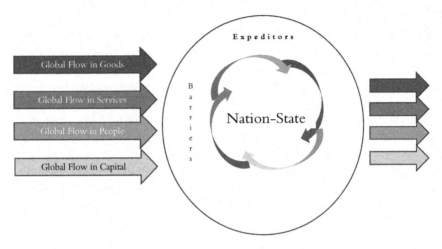

FIGURE 2.1 Global flows framework

Barriers and expeditors

There are **Barriers** that restrict or inhibit Global Flows, and **Expeditors** that facilitate their movements (see Figure 2.1). The decades following the end of the Second World War saw a proliferation of multilateral agencies (UN, IMF, World Bank, WTO) and international treaties like the GATT, GATS, TRIPS[8] and the Lisbon Treaty (which underpins the current form of the European Union) among others.[9] So, our claim that Barriers and Expeditors are essentially national may be a little counterintuitive. A significant portion of the globalization discourse over the last few decades has been about how nations have 'lost' sovereignty, how their decision-making powers have drained away to multilateral bodies. But this is a rather one-sided interpretation of the events. Nation-states choose to join multilateral agencies and sign international treaties because they serve their own interests. The UK chose to become a member of the EU, and now has decided to relinquish that membership.[10] National governments decide to what extent they want to be integrated with the rest of the globe. The Netherlands is the most connected country in the world according to the Global Connectedness Index.[11] Sudan is the least connected. The reasons why the connectedness of these two countries differ widely have to do with their respective national histories and government policies. This is what we mean when we say that Barriers and Expeditors are essentially national in character.

A nation-state can reduce Global Flows by erecting Barriers and increase their velocity by creating Expeditors. Membership of the European Single Market is an Expeditor. Capital controls are a Barrier. Globally connected countries experience high levels of Global Flows, which are in turn impacted by their national Barriers and Expeditors. These countries typically have few Barriers and many Expeditors. The opposite is true for countries that are cut-off from Global Flows. It is important to keep in mind that Global Flows often act as double-edged swords;

they can help and hurt a country. Global Flows have undoubtedly brought prosperity to many countries[12], but they have also heightened the level of uncertainty within the economy.[13] National level differences in Barriers and Expeditors affect the velocity of circulation of Global Flows within respective economies. Some nation-states are more open to Global Flows than others; the reasons for such differences in policymaking can be both ideological and historical. The velocity of Global Flows also varies across industries. It is entirely possible within an economy to have an insulated sector and another very open one. In the UK, the financial industry is more open to Global Flows than the heath sector, so their dynamics would vary accordingly.

How to think about uncertainty

The macro environment has become uncertain and disruptive due to the twin forces of globalization and digitization (see Case study 2.2 on digitization). But uncertainty is a topic that is generally avoided in strategy textbooks. The reasons for this are not hard to fathom. Strategic thinking is dominated by what we call the planning paradigm – the idea that the future can be predicted, and strategy is about devising a roadmap to maximize profits in that future world.[14] It is not used to the idea that increased complexity makes long-term planning a much less useful exercise than before. We argue here that strategic thinking in the twenty-first century must incorporate uncertainty, making it a core element of any conceptual apparatus.

Risk and uncertainty

Uncertainty and Risk: in popular business literature, the two terms are often used as synonyms, but conceptually, a distinction between the two can be easily made.[15] Simply put, 'Risk' is a possible adverse future event that you can insure against. If you build a house on the flood plains, the chances are that your house is going to be flooded sometime in the near or distant future. You can protect yourself against this negative future event by purchasing a home insurance. You pay extra premium for the higher risk, but you are insured against potential flooding. Any future scenario against which it is possible to assign the probability of its occurrence, can be considered as Risk. Risky events have a past, and that past data help us to estimate how likely it is that a similar event will occur in the future.

Uncertainty, on the other hand, is uninsurable. If there is no historical regularity of a particular event, the chances of it happening in the future cannot be predicted in probabilistic terms. Think of any technological innovation. Its success depends on so many variable factors – the usefulness of the new technology, reliability, acceptance of users, viability of the business model and access to markets. With so many variables, it is impossible to estimate its success ex-ante in probabilistic terms. Businesses do insure against some risks, but the core of any business in a competitive market is uninsurable.

The entrepreneur, unlike the homeowner, is comfortable with uninsurable uncertainty precisely because the payoff is also uncertain – there can be debilitating losses but also huge rewards. In 2018, the British Library organized an exhibition titled 'Harry Potter: A History of Magic'.[16] This was to celebrate the twentieth anniversary of the publication of *Harry Potter and the Philosopher's Stone*. The book is the third bestselling book of all time with 120 million copies sold worldwide. But the book's manuscript was rejected twelve times before a little-known publisher at the time, Bloomsbury, agreed to publish it. So, twelve professional publishing houses failed to see the potential of the third bestselling book of all time! This fact underlines the uncertainty in payoffs of innovation. J. K. Rowling, the author of the Harry Potter series, was not disheartened by the rejections because she was convinced of the quality of her work. She was comfortable with the uncertainty, and the big payoff made up for the small losses encountered earlier, multiple times over. J. K. Rowling is by no means the only creator/entrepreneur who encountered failure before tasting success; numerous other entrepreneurs have had similar experiences although perhaps not at the same scale.

The point we are making here is that disruptive uncertainty, the defining feature of the current business landscape, signifies both risk and opportunities for companies. But this also means that simplistic prediction-based analytical tools like PEST are of limited value to firms in their search for profits. We need new conceptual tools that take uncertainty seriously. We present one such framework in Chapter 7 (Creating options).

CASE STUDY 2.1: GLOBALIZATION – THE NETHERLANDS

On 19 May 2019, Duncan de Moor, better known with his artist's name Duncan Laurence, won the Eurovision Song festival in Tel Aviv with his song 'Arcade'.[1] In one of the verses he describes himself as a 'small-town boy in a big arcade'.

To a small-town boy born in Spijkenisse, a town just across the Old Maas river to the south-west of Rotterdam, Mr de Moor must have obtained an early impression of a construction of a much bigger proportion.

Covering a total area of 127 square kilometres (almost 79 square miles) of land and sea, over a total length of 42 km (26 miles), the Port of Rotterdam is currently Europe's biggest port and ranked eleventh of the world's biggest container ports. In 2018, the Port of Rotterdam handled 77.6 million tonnes of dry bulk goods, 211.8 million tonnes of liquid bulk goods and 149.1 million tonnes of container cargo.[2]

The DHL Global Connectedness Index for 2018 ranks The Netherlands first of the globally connected countries – out of 169 countries. The report illustrates that the country's top slot was achieved by a combination of large flows of international trade activities – relative to the size of the country's economy – with a broad range of destination countries.[3]

Historically, The Netherlands has deeply established trade relations with its neighbouring countries. Going back to 1957, The Netherlands was for example one of the six founding countries of the European Economic Community (EEC), which later became the European Union (EU).[4] With a view to the sea and the country's heritage in colonial sea-trade, The Netherlands translated some of its historical experiences into a view on the future that appears remarkably sustainable.

The lead position as a globally connected country is based on a variety of elements possessed by The Netherlands. Any attempt to provide a conclusive analysis of its rank would probably fall short, as there are many pitfalls. However, four elements are worth mentioning that may help us to better understand how the country achieved its position.

First is the role played by the country's logistical infrastructure and transportation facilities. The logistical infrastructure is integrated along sea- and airports and extends towards transportation facilities by train, vessels and lorries. As such, logistical services provide a critical contribution to the country's economy as the Port of Rotterdam illustrates. Additionally, related industry sectors that contribute to the country's position in global production chains comprise for example, the processing facilities of imported bulk goods that surround harbours and airports. Around 10% of the Dutch gross domestic product (GDP) relates directly to logistical services.[5]

The second element that contributes to the country's connectedness relates to the financial and professional service infrastructure in facilitating international activities. The Netherlands is not only connected through tangible product flows on an international scale. The country also facilitates intangible financial and business transactions as well as trade-services and insurances. As such, the position of The Netherlands in international business is based on a range of professional and corporate service firms. Supportive business regulation and commercial law plays an equally important role. As such, a World Bank report issued in 2016, emphasized the efficiency and effectiveness of the country's customs and border procedures in its role to promote international trade.[6]

A third element that adds to the country's position includes the role of information technology infrastructure. IT-infrastructure and related services help to facilitate the integration of service activities on a global level. The World Bank report mentioned above also points towards the role of critical IT infrastructure as a relevant element of the country's competitive position. Another industry report, issued by the Federation of Dutch Data Centers illustrates, furthermore, that around one-quarter of the country's GDP depends on services relating to data centres.[7] This may come as no surprise, given the dependency of global services and the role communication infrastructure plays within the broader realm of international commercial activities.

The fourth element is based on the country's spatial position as a relatively small sea-nation; there are still some traces of its history in merchant trade in the current conditions of the economy and society. Many Dutch citizens, for example, have ancestral roots in the former colonies of the Dutch East Indies (now comprising areas of Indonesia), in South America (now Suriname) or the Dutch Caribbean Islands. In the past, the state monopoly for sea-trade with the Dutch East Indies was granted to the Verenigde Oostindische Company (VOC), as 'The Canon of the Netherlands' illustrates.[8] The VOC is also the world's first corporation to issue company shares to the public.

Therefore, The Netherlands did not only deploy international sea-trade, it also invented a form of company financing that had the potential to develop into a global phenomenon in its own right – the stock exchange listed public corporation.

The picture that emerges out of the various elements may easily be summarized as an idiosyncratic framework of global connectivity. It is not a single element that caused The Netherlands to develop into a globally connected nation. Hence, it is rather a range of factors that contribute to the global connectiveness of The Netherlands. To many Dutch 'small-town boy(s)' – and girls, living in a globally connected country is the traditional way of living.

Sources

[1] Duncan Laurance – official website: https://duncanlaurence.nl
[2] Port of Rotterdam – official website: www.portofrotterdam.com/en
[3] DHL Global Connectedness Index 2018 on The Netherlands: www.dpdhl.com/en/media-relations/specials/global-connectedness-index.html
[4] History of the European Union – official website: https://europa.eu/european-union/about-eu/history_en
[5] The Holland International Distribution Council – official website: https://hollandinternationaldistributioncouncil.com/en/
[6] The World Bank – official website: www.worldbank.org/en/country/netherlands/overview
[7] Dutch Federation of Data Center – official website: www.dutchdatacenters.nl
[8] The Canon of The Netherlands on the VOC – official website: www.entoen.nu/nl/voc

Case study 2.2: 'Digitalization of everything' – the banking industry Background and introduction

Global banking is one of the most interesting sectors of the world economy. The ups and downs of the global economy play out via this sector of critical importance, both for businesses and individuals. The sector consists of 25,000 fully licensed banks[1] globally. In Q3 2019, the sector had total assets of US$124 trillion[2] and market capitalization of approximately US$8 trillion.[3] The recent advent of 'Digital everything' is an opportunity for banks to increase adoption of innovative technology to reduce risk, improve efficiency and improve the customer offer as well as leverage such digital channels to provide personalized products and services to an enlarged base of customers. Globally, 3 billion users will be covered by digital-powered banking in 2021.[4]

The following pages in this case study use this important sector as an example to illustrate the transformative trend of the 'Digitalization of everything'.

Two important factors are driving this change:

1. Radical shifts in customer behaviour, demanding unprecedented speed and instant convenience of 'digital' rather than 'physical' transactions. Consumers want to do their banking at their convenience, at a time and place of their choice rather than stand in bank branch queues for hours.
2. Exponential improvements in computing power and global communications infrastructure coupled with new technologies are facilitating high levels of internal automation, data-driven product development and highly engaged customer experiences.

Global technology companies are making forays into banking; for example Amazon with its financial services, Apple with its Cards and Apple Pay, and Ant financial (affiliate of Chinese e-commerce Alibaba group) with Alipay, MYbank, etc.

As a recent report from IBM[5] mentions:

> Financial services are being mixed in with services or products from other areas and industries, and banking is becoming embedded – sometimes almost invisibly – in non-bank business processes. New types of ecosystems are developing, powered by dynamic new business models, often based around platforms and network economics.

Banking: Harnessing tactical change for strategic advantage

In the 1970s and 1980s, the big trend in this industry was digitizing data and processes for higher operational efficiencies, improving profitability and freeing up expensive human resources for higher value-add activities.

Digitization was a narrow resource-based activity, that essentially took analogue information and converted it into a digital form of zeroes and ones that could be processed faster, predictably and more accurately by machines. The process of IT outsourcing in the 1980s to external firms was hugely popular with the top tier investment banks (JP Morgan, State Street, Barclays Capital), as also with the Western headquartered banks with large networks and branches in Asia and Africa (Citibank, HSBC, Standard Chartered).

The next phase of change in banking was in the late 1990s and early 2000s. It was the advent of Digitized Operating Models where the data as well as process underwent digital transformation, typically in purpose-built operations subsidiaries called 'Captive Centers' or at service providers located on-shore, near-shore or off-shore (defined as proximity to the parent company).

These digitized processes created new opportunities for interactions not only inside the organization but with external partnerships and service providers. This was the age of the BPO or business process outsourcing that aimed to enhance the efficiency and cost-effectiveness of a company's operations.

The play in this phase was cost reductions via labour arbitrage and talent acquisition of educated, English-speaking and skilled workforce available in the developing Asian and, to some extent, Eastern European ex-Soviet-bloc economies.

In this decade of disruption, however, that change has morphed to a much-larger revolution that is hyper-charged by technology. 'Digitalization' is now paving the way for new business models and new business imperatives, where customers are being served with new products and services, produced internally or in partnership with an 'ecosystem' and delivered via new channels including portable and wearable devices in a globally borderless marketplace.

Digitalization is a fundamental rethinking of the business that Gartner defines as 'use of digital technologies to change a business model that produces new revenue and value-producing opportunities'.[6]

Disruption as a source for creating competitive advantage: Banking industry example

Finally, the Janus-faced characteristic of disruption is showcased via examples of innovative startups in the finance industry that are harnessing the positive forces of globalization and disruption, as well as older incumbents that are re-imagining their businesses to competitively respond, survive and thrive.

We illustrate this with an example of each category. An example of the first category is a disruptive startup called N26, a direct digital-only retail bank in Europe that is just five years old but has a valuation of $3.5 billion (July 2019). The example of the other category is PayPal (revenues of $16 billion, valuation of nearly $100 billion, 2018), which is a Fortune 500 financial payments provider founded in 1998, and is now a competitor to many retail and commercial incumbents in the 500-year-old banking industry as well as to many payment-focused providers across the globe.

N26 – A digital bank going global

N26 is a typical example of how competitive advantage can be created, simply, with the new opportunities that the world of digitalization now offers.

Its proposition leverages on the booming use of smartphones by the new digital-hungry world population, but primarily consisting of Millennials, Generation X, Y, Z and later. Their clear message of 'Run your entire financial life from your phone' and 'You never have to visit a bank again' is simple, clear and concise.

Simply put, N26 is a basic banking account linked to a smartphone and a card, but it typifies the finance industry of the future, where digital-led 'challenger' banks and innovative financial technology or 'fintech' companies are challenging the existence of the conventional banking and finance industry. N26 started its life in Germany and Austria as a current account with a Mastercard. It now operates as a fully featured bank, serving customers in 24 European markets, the UK, Switzerland and US, with plans to expand in Brazil soon.

The nearly 4 million customers of N26 sign up from their phones and get a card that can be controlled from a phone with the freedom to spend all around the world without any foreign transaction fees.

The power of 'Digital' is creating an endless supply of innovative consumer-centric propositions which offer cheaper, faster, more convenient services to the end-user.

'Digitalization of everything' is unbundling products and services in ways that are affecting the fundamental business models of the banking industry. Both retail and institutional banks are being impacted by Fintech, which is a digitalized banking industry hyper-charged by use of new technologies. Fintech is being driven by an abundance of cheap and commanding computing power, a superfast communication infrastructure that includes smartphones, and the omnipresent internet that is lowering barriers of entry into business sectors such as banking by harnessing global innovation.

As a result, it is the consumer or end-user who is reaping benefits from the ensuing fierce competition that is spawning an immense choice of banking and related services.

As in the past, customers do not need to remain beholden to one 'big bank' that serves all their financial needs. They are able to get a personalized array of services which they can use at a convenient time and place to suit their lifestyles rather than having to stand in long queues in bank branches of crowded city centres.

Digitalization is the underlying enabler. The two founders of N26, Valentin Stalf and Maximilian Tayenthal, state that they are building a retail bank that simply 'works better'. 'We are a technology company with a banking license'.

That is the underlying premise of competitive advantage for digital challenger brands in financial services that use technology to delight their targeted customer base with factors like simplicity, ease of use and convenience built around customers' lifestyles.

Newer digital entrants put a superlative customer experience at the heart of the customer proposition. This value proposition is clearly and simply articulated on their home page rather than as a complicated suite of products and services embalmed in the difficult jargon of most older brick-and-mortar bank websites. Digital banks like N26 also tend to be more specifically targeted to specific segments of customers, which in the case of N26, is the prolific smartphone user for whom a superior online experience is more important than any offline experience. This is made possible through use of hyper-personalization using smart data, AI, 5G and new cloud technologies.

New generation digital players like N26 have another intrinsic competitive advantage. They are untainted by reputational misdemeanours of the past by established industry incumbents – for example PPI mis-selling in the UK or the Wells Fargo account fraud in the USA – and don't have to expend the effort of re-building trust, transparency and fairness in customers.

In addition to the customer-facing advantages that full digital banks like N26 enjoy, they threaten the existence of traditional players with a structural advantage of paramount importance: associated cost of service provision. A recent study found that, depending on each user profile, digital banks are between two and four times less expensive to run than the cheapest traditional banks.[7]

Armed with that structural advantage of a cost differential in running a banking business that provided elemental competitive advantage, digitization in banks is now enhancing the full value chain of the bank's customer offer in all aspects. The areas encompassed are:

1. Enhanced banking functionalities (e.g. standing orders with variable conditions)
2. Improvements in account utilities (e.g. yield enhanced savings accounts)
3. Consolidating household banking data (e.g. family accounts from different banks)
4. Community interaction tools (e.g. forum to discuss with other customers, peer to peer investing)
5. 24x7x365 virtual assistance (e.g. intelligent chatbots, robo advisors)

It is, however, really customer evolution and customer behaviour that is driving the re-imagination of banks' customer interaction models. The complete customer journey in retail banking is being digitized, and every component of that journey given below is being affected:

1. Onboarding of new customers
2. Design of customer experiences
3. Delivery of content and functionality
4. Ergonomics of technology use
5. Customer touch points
6. Security of money and data
7. Advice
8. Credit and loans

9. Travel and international transactions
10. Account closing

As one example, N26 boasts a '8-minute' account opening target the moment a customer starts interaction on its site.

Here are six new-generation features of the N26 banking account that are enabled by digital:[10]

1. Fee-free cash withdrawals worldwide

You can withdraw cash as often as you want and wherever you want free of charge. It only matters that the ATM accepts Mastercard, as do most ATMs worldwide.

2. Free international transactions and payments in foreign currencies

There are no fees for use outside the account holder's home country. Transactions in other currencies are converted directly without extra fees, using Mastercard's exchange rate.

3. Control-centre with card blocking options

The customer can activate or deactivate the credit card for particular regions via the mobile banking app or online banking; for example to prohibit use abroad. This feature disables a credit card from fraudulent usage or withdrawals abroad. The feature can be activated during personal travel abroad.

A variety of options are provided:

• Blocking of payments abroad
• Blocking of payments on the internet
• Blocking of usage at ATMs
• Complete blocking of the credit card

With these features, N26 gives people the greatest possible freedom and personal responsibility.

4. Money Beam – instant money transfers

With Money Beam, customers can simply send money to people on their contact list (smartphone) without having to remember or enter other cumbersome details like bank routing codes or 35-digit IBAN numbers. Transfers happen within the same day, and for payees with N26 accounts, the money will be transferred immediately.

5. Push notifications for each account movement

Account holders receive push notifications for all transactions **in real time** on their smartphone. This reduces the incidence of fraud, and allows higher visibility for planning individual finances, for example, when a salary payment comes into your account.

6. Analysis

N26 regularly provides its customers with several analytical indicators and metrics on account usage, income, expenditure, savings patterns and spending behaviour. All banking transactions are processed automatically into categories, which the customer also has the flexibility to modify. Pictorial indicators help its customers to understand and optimize their financial life-style, and identify savings opportunities.

N26 is an example of a banking account in the new digital economy that offers ultimate flexibility, convenience and value to the customer using the power of technology.

One thing is clear – digitization of everything is being driven in the retail banking industry as two-thirds of customers now do most of their banking online.[9] Add to this the emergence of digital native customer base of the newer generation of customers, and it is evident that structural change is emerging in the behaviours of banking customers.

The experiences of several banks worldwide show that adding 'digital capabilities' to an existing banking business model does not create the step change to meet customer needs and sustain commercial profitability. For example, digital newcomers and challenger banks have captured one-third of all revenue growth in Europe in the last 2 years (2018/19).[10] Banks have to adopt digital business models to compete and thrive in this economy.

References

1. The Accuity Bankers Almanac lists data of 25,000 banks. Additionally, there are 60,000 quasi-banks that include community credit unions, co-operatives, savings associations, building societies, etc.
2. The Banker Top 1000 World Banks ranking for 2018.
3. The Banker, World Banking report 2019.
4. Juniper Research: www.juniperresearch.com/press/press-releases/digital-banking-users-reach-nearly-3-billion-2021
5. IBM – Banking in a platform economy, October 2019.
6. Gartner – Digital Technology as change.
7. Les offres des banques internet au banc d'essai, Agnes Lambert, 2017.
8. Study of digital banks in Luxembourg.
9. Accenture 2019 report – New arrivals re-arrange the banking sky.
10. N26 product coverage in Banking Technology Media.

Conclusion

As we have seen in this chapter, owing to the twin disruptors – digitization and globalization – the macro environment has become more uncertain than ever before.
In such a situation, long-term planning is fraught with difficulties. Yet, firms do
need to make long-term investments and to effect that they necessarily must take
a view on the future – how it is likely to pan out. In Chapter 7, we discuss how
firms can not only cope but flourish in a context where the macro environment is
hyper-uncertain.

This is not to say that there is no value in conventional strategic management
ideas. Much of the conventional literature does not assume that decision makers
are hyperrational. But some of it does, especially when it comes to thinking about
the macro environment. This chapter has shown why in these disruptive times that
approach may be ill-suited.

Notes

1 Please see Mintzberg et al., 1998.
2 See Friedman's lecture, available at https://youtu.be/kev-MvZlm_g.
3 Global Flows is a powerful way of conceptualizing the globalization process. For a good
  exposition of the idea of Global Flows from the sociological perspective, see George
  Ritzer's *Globalization: The Essentials*, 2011.
4 An overview of such trades can be found at this link: www.khanacademy.org/
  humanities/world-history/world-history-beginnings/ancient-india/a/the-indus-
  river-valley-civilizations.
5 See https://markets.businessinsider.com/news/stocks/most-valuable-tech-companies-
  total-worth-trillions-alphabet-stock-record-2020-1-1028826533.
6 See for example the executive order issued by Donald Trump, President of the United
  States, reprimanding online censorship practised by social media companies. Without
  getting into the merits of the order, we can safely say that this demonstrates conclusively
  the private ownership of virtual public space. The executive order can be accessed at this
  link: www.whitehouse.gov/presidential-actions/executive-order-preventing-online-
  censorship/.
7 See Gupta and Govindarajan, 2000.
8 GATT (General Agreement on Tariffs and Trade), GATS (General Agreement on Trade
  in Services) and TRIPS (Trade-related Aspects of Intellectual Property Rights) are international treaties that regulate trade in goods, services and intellectual properties. These
  three treaties form the main pillars of the WTO (World Trade Organization).
9 For an overview of multilateralism in the post-Second World War period, see Van
  Langenhove, 2010.
10 The UK voted to leave the EU in the EU Referendum held in 2016.
11 The report on DHL Global Connected Index can be accessed at this link: www.dpdhl.
  com/en/media-relations/specials/global-connectedness-index.html.
12 For a good overview of the debate around the benefits of international trade, see Lin and
  Chang, 2009.

13 Short-term capital flows in and out of a country can create huge instabilities in the economy. The East Asian financial crisis of the late 1990s is a prime example of this. For an explanation of the origins of the crisis, see Rajan and Zingales, 1998.
14 Also see Mintzberg et al., 1998.
15 The distinction was first made by Frank Knight in his 1921 classic *Risk, Uncertainty, and Profit*.
16 The British Library page on the exhibition can be found at this link: www.bl.uk/a-history-of-magic/articles/a-brief-history-of-magic.

Further reading

Barney, J. (1991). Firm resources and sustained competitive advantage. *Journal of management*, 17(1), 99–120.

Friedman, T. L. (2006). *The world is flat [updated and expanded]: A brief history of the twenty-first century*. New York: Macmillan.

Gupta, A. K., & Govindarajan, V. (2000). Knowledge flows within multinational corporations. *Strategic management journal*, 21(4), 473–496.

Knight, F. H. (1921). *Risk, uncertainty and profit*. New York: Harper & Row.

Lin, J., & Chang, H. J. (2009). Should industrial policy in developing countries conform to comparative advantage or defy it? A debate between Justin Lin and Ha-Joon Chang. *Development policy review*, 27(5), 483–502.

Mintzberg, H., Ahlstrand, B., & Lampel, J. (1998). *Strategy safari: A guided tour through the wilds of strategic management*. New York: Free Press.

Ohmae, K. (1989). Managing in a borderless world. *Harvard business review*, 67(3), 152–161.

Rajan, R. G., & Zingales, L. (1998). Which capitalism? Lessons from the East Asian crisis. *Journal of applied corporate finance*, 11(3), 40–48.

Ritzer, G. (2011). *Globalisation: The essentials*. New York: John Wiley & Sons.

Ritzer, G., & Dean, P. (2015). *Globalization: A basic text*. Chichester: Wiley Blackwell.

Teece, D. J., Pisano, G., & Shuen, A. (1997). Dynamic capabilities and strategic management. *Strategic management journal*, 18(7), 509–533.

Van Langenhove, L. (2010). The transformation of multilateralism mode 1.0 to mode 2.0. *Global policy*, 1(3), 263–270.

3

RESOURCES

Assets, capabilities and strategic positioning

Resources are key to survival. We cannot survive without water, food, housing and clothes. But we want to do more than survive, we want to prosper and flourish. Successful people have control of or access to better resources – higher education, surplus capital for investment, a safe neighbourhood to live in, a supportive spouse, a valuable social network, and so on.

What is true for people is also true for firms. All firms need resources to survive, but firms that have a competitive advantage usually have access to superior assets compared to their rivals. This chapter is about understanding what these resources are and how they are deployed in the real word by firms to generate competitive advantage.

Tangible and intangible resources

One popular way of conceptualizing organizational resources is to classify them into **tangible** and **intangible resources**.

Examples of tangible resources are:

a. Buildings
b. Land
c. Capital (machineries)
d. Cash and financial investment

Examples of intangible resources are:

a. Brand
b. Intellectual properties (such as patents and copyrights)
c. Goodwill
d. Trademarks

The resource-based view of competitive advantage

The extant literature on competitive advantage can be broadly divided into two schools of thought. The first is the resource-based view of the firm (or the RBV of competitive advantage) which we will discuss in this section. The other, the Structure-Conduct-Performance (S-C-P) paradigm is discussed later in the chapter. The main idea of RBV is that the source of competitive advantage of firms is to be found inside its boundaries. This differs from the S-C-P paradigm which holds that the industry is the source of organizational competitive advantage.

Capabilities

A distinction can be made between resources and capabilities. Capabilities are ways in which resources are used by the company.[1] To carry out an activity, several resources are deployed. Within any industry, rivals may own similar kinds of resources, but the patterns of their usage may radically differ from each other. Capabilities are patterns of organizational activities. They are routines that firms have established to perform specific tasks. As an example, research and development can be considered a capability rather than a resource. Companies carry out R&D activities to come up with new products, deploying organizational resources like R&D staff and research laboratories. These patterns of activities are specific to a firm; they are never identical even within an industry that has players dealing in identical products. Organizational routines can be thought of as memories of the firm. These established patterns of activities are how things get done within the organization. **Organizational assets** then would include both firm specific resources and capabilities.

So, what kinds of organizational assets are more important for competitive success? Tangible or intangible? The answer here is pretty straightforward – both. You may have a particular machinery that your competitor does not have, or the location of your business is far superior to your competitors' – examples of tangible resources. Alternatively, the source of competitive success may be its brand, the goodwill a firm enjoys, or a particular patent that the firm owns – all examples of intangible resources.

Unique resources and capabilities of the firm

RBV enthusiasts argue that the main source of any competitive advantage is those bundles of resources and capabilities that are unique to the firm.[2] This point of view essentially stems from economics which equates rarity or scarcity with value. As unique organizational assets are by definition specific to the firm, they are rare, hence they are valuable and as a consequence they create organizational value or, in other words, competitive success.

But not everything that is scarce or rare is valuable. A firm may own a patent (something specific to the firm, hence rare) which does not have any commercial application. So, how can we determine unique resources and capabilities that are truly valuable?

Unique and threshold assets

One way to classify organizational assets is by making the uniqueness or threshold distinction. Some organizational assets such as resources and capabilities, are critical for competitive advantage – these **unique assets** are specific to the firm; its competitors cannot own them. **Threshold assets** on the other hand are those bundles of resources and competences that every player in the industry needs to have to survive as a competitor. Survival is different from flourishing. Threshold assets are required for survival. Unique assets are needed for flourishing.

It is obvious that the list of threshold assets is going to be lot longer than that of unique assets. Indeed, it may be the case that some competitors in the market do not really have unique assets, their portfolio being made up of entirely threshold assets. These players would typically generate industry average or below industry average profitability. On the other hand, it would be odd if a particular firm in an industry consistently outperforms its rivals, yet does not own anything 'special', which gives it the edge over its competitors. If unique assets are at the root of competitive success, then not all firms have them, as not all firms have competitive advantage.

Defining competitive advantage

We have already mentioned competitive advantage quite a few times in this chapter, but we have not defined it yet. So, before we go further with our discussion on unique resources and how they contribute to competitive advantage, let's first understand what the term means. We have already said that not all players within an industry have competitive advantage. One way to identify these firms, to separate the wheat from the chaff as the saying goes, is by looking at the profitability figures of the industry players over time. Take a profitability indicator like return on sales or return on investment. Looking at all the competitors within an industry, it is possible to compute the industry average profitability. Firms with genuine competitive advantage should be outperforming the industry average profitability.[3] It is important to take a long-term perspective. It is relatively easy to outperform the industry average in one particular year, it is however much more difficult to do so consistently over a 10-year time frame. So, there are two key dimensions to competitive advantage: first, a superior performance vis-à-vis industry averages and, second, that superiority needs to be maintained over the long term.

Identification of unique or core assets

If you accept the premise that competitive success rests primarily on unique resources, or, as it is sometimes called, core assets, then the question which naturally

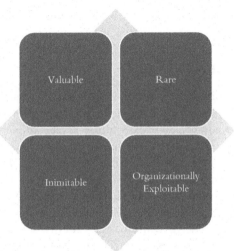

FIGURE 3.1 Identification of core assets

arises is – how do you identify them? The VRIO framework (see Barney, 1995), the main pillar of the RBV school, strives to provide the answer. To qualify as 'unique' an asset must meet the following criteria (see Figure 3.1):

It must be **V**aluable
It must be **R**are
It must be **I**nimitable
It must be **O**rganizationally exploitable.

Let's take each of these by turn.

Valuable: For an asset to be valuable, its link to the firm's competitive advantage should be clear. If a product innovation is based on a patent, the latter is a valuable organizational resource. Toyota's production system directly feeds into its competitive success; hence it qualifies as a valuable asset.

Rare: This may sound obvious – how can a unique asset *not* be rare? If it is widely available, then it cannot be unique to the firm. However, even for a resource that is widely available within the industry, its rarity arises out of the way that it is deployed within the firm. A football manager may be wildly successful in one team, yet he may find it difficult to replicate that success in another team even with greater financial resources at his disposal. The rarity of the resource, such as our football manager in this case, is context dependent.

Inimitable: For a resource to be inimitable there must be some barriers to copying it by the firm's rivals. RBV scholars suggest that 'causal ambiguity' is the main barrier to imitation. Simply put, causal ambiguity exists when the link between resources and competitive advantage is not clear; no one knows for sure which organizational assets are critical to the firm's success.

Organizationally exploitable: A company may have a valuable resource yet may choose not to exploit it. Many of the path-breaking inventions of the Palo Alto Research Centre (PARC) of Xerox were not exploited by the firm itself but by others. This was either done through licensing or by ex-employees setting up companies themselves. So, for a resource to deliver competitive success it needs to be exploited effectively. This may sound obvious, but we can provide many examples, similar to PARC, of companies missing out on exploiting valuable organizational resources.

Problems with RBV

Identification of Uniqueness: Causal ambiguity means the link between the resources and competitive advantage is not clear, not only to outsiders but even to the people within the organization itself.[4] In the presence of causal ambiguity, you can never be sure that the resources that have been identified as 'unique' really contribute to the competitive success of the firm. Also, there is an element of circular reasoning in RBV. The resources are identified as valuable because they are eventually found to be valuable, hence contributing to competitive success. It can explain competitive success but cannot be a guide to strategic action that leads to that outcome.

Static analysis

A key drawback of RBV is that it is a static analysis. An RBV analysis is a snapshot of the firm's assets at a point in time. But the competitive environment is constantly evolving. The valuable resources and capabilities of today may be the threshold assets of tomorrow; in other words, the minimum required to become a player in the industry. In the worst-case scenario, today's valuable assets can actively work against a firm's competitive advantage in the future; in other words, hinder you to remain a player in your industry.

Think of Blockbuster, the video rental firm. At its peak it had over 9,000 stores across the globe which were essential to its business model. Its superior network of video rental stores was, in fact, its source of competitive advantage over its rivals. It was much easier for customers to borrow and then return DVDs to Blockbuster stores as one was just around the corner. Yet, with the advent of Netflix and other on-demand streaming services, this unique organizational asset of Blockbuster, its superior network of physical stores, became an albatross around its neck, dragging its profitability down.

So, the RBV framework can be useful to analyse why the firm has been successful in the past; it cannot act as a guide to strategic action that is geared towards the future. This also brings us to the point we made in Chapter 2. The disruptive uncertainty in the environment is making traditional strategic management tools less effective. The pace of change is simultaneously exhilarating and exhausting. For a firm like Blockbuster, sustaining competitive advantage meant rejecting everything that made it a success in previous years, and reinventing itself. Not surprisingly, it failed. Very few firms have been able to transform their core activities within a rapidly evolving environment.

Dynamic capabilities

There has been an attempt within the RBV school itself to address the critique that it is a static analysis. A way out of the quagmire was found through the notion of **dynamic capabilities**.[5] The suggestion here is that firms need to have separate kinds of capabilities that are focused on reconfiguring their existing capabilities considering the ever-changing external environment.[6] Dynamic capabilities are decomposed into two separate sub-capabilities – **sensing** and **seizing**. Sensing is about understanding how the external environment is changing, while Seizing is about taking strategic action to counter the threats and exploit the opportunities arising out of that situation. Sensing is scanning the environment; Seizing is taking strategic action.

Of course, the concept of dynamic capabilities seems neat on paper, executing it in practice is a different matter altogether. Not many organizations seem to be able to successfully transform their core activities, resources and capabilities over time. This is particularly true for successful firms. If you are successful, you tend to think that the recipe for success is going to last forever, not realizing that the success of the recipe is context dependent. Business history is full of cases of seemingly invincible companies vanishing from the landscape almost overnight.[7] Longevity is a key indicator of the presence of dynamic capabilities. After casting an appraising glance over the landscape, we must come to the unmistakable conclusion that very few companies over the course of history have had dynamic capabilities. IBM is one company that has been able to transform itself from a manufacturing firm to an organization that is service oriented. But for one IBM there are a thousand others that have chosen to stick to their knitting and failed as a consequence.

It is worth noting here that the idea of dynamic capabilities assumes certain foresight on the part of the organization. The company's sensing capabilities are essentially about forecasting how the future is going to unfold. It raises the question – how well can they forecast such changes when the environment is fraught with disruptive uncertainty? We revisit this issue in Chapter 7, 'Creating options'.

Strategic positioning

There are essentially two schools of thought in strategic management. The **'inside out'** and the **'outside in'** approaches. We have already discussed the 'inside out' approach – the resource-based view of the firm. This approach subscribes to the general idea that the source of competitive advantage lies inside the boundaries of the firm. It is to be found in its routines, capabilities, resources and combinations thereof. The view gained popularity in the last couple of decades of the twentieth century and still remains *en vogue* today. The 'outside in' approach predates the 'inside out' one. It has its origins in industrial organization, a sub-discipline in economics. It is sometimes referred to as the **Structure–Conduct–Performance (SCP) paradigm.**[8] The main idea is that the structure of the industry guides individual firm strategy (conduct) which subsequently delivers the performance (profitability). Think about the patented drug industry. Here, the industry dynamics determine that any competitive player would need to invest in R&D to develop new patented drugs which are its basis of profitability.

Industry analysis

Under the 'outside-in' approach, strategy making starts from an industry analysis. Within the business landscape there are attractive and unattractive industries. Strategy is about **positioning** your organization within attractive industry sectors and getting out of or avoiding unattractive markets. To evaluate industry attractiveness, the well-known **5 Forces Framework** (see Porter, 2008b) can be used. The framework (see Figure 3.2) specifies the key drivers of industry attractiveness – the power of buyers, the power of sellers, the threat of new entrants, the threat of substitutes and the intensity of competitive rivalry. An industry, or industry sector, where all the 5 forces are high, is an unattractive proposition.

Think of the airlines industry. With the advent of internet bookings, we, as buyers, can browse for the cheapest fare. Airline seats are perishable commodities,

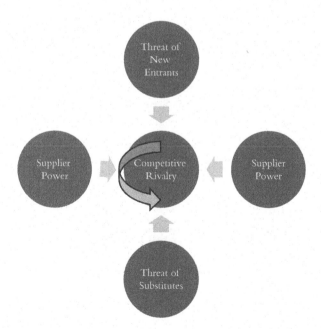

FIGURE 3.2 Porter's 5 forces

the value of an empty seat immediately becomes zero as soon as the aircraft has left its docking station at the airport. As there is no switching cost for us to transfer our allegiance from one airline to the other, our bargaining power is relatively high. The power of sellers, the aircraft manufacturers like Boeing and Airbus, is also high because there are few of them and airlines typically lease the aircrafts from them on a long-term basis. Short distance airlines face threats of substitutes from alternative means of transport such as bus, train and car. For long distance airlines, the threat of substitutes is relatively lower, but here too, with improvements in communication technologies, people can sometimes avoid travelling and interact virtually. The competitive rivalry within the airline industry is very high, with many airlines fighting for the market that has been more or less stagnant over the last few decades. The threat of new entrants is high because the airline industry is not capital intensive, unlike the aircraft industry which is hugely capital intensive. As all the 5 forces are high in relation to the airline industry, the assessment is that it is a highly unattractive industry.

On the other hand, if we look at the patented pharmaceutical sector, all the 5 forces are either low or moderate:

- high entry barriers, such as R&D capability and capital intensity, signify a low threat of new entrants,
- competitive rivalry is low as drugs are patented and hence cannot be copied,
- low power of sellers as generic chemicals are used in production,
- low power of buyers as specific drugs are owned by individual firms so switching cost is high, and
- threat of substitutes is moderate to low.

Thus, bio-tech has the potential to be a real threat in the future, but its current impact is not very significant. So, the patented pharmaceutical sector, evaluated through the 5 forces framework, will be considered an attractive industry.

It is also possible to have different **Strategic Groups** (see Caves and Porter, 1977) within a particular industry. Strategic groups emerge as firms choose to have different competitive strategies. Within the strategic groups, firms tend to pursue similar strategies, which differ from those practised within another strategic group. In the following section, these different strategies are explained.

Generic strategies

Once you have identified the industry that is worth competing in, based on high profitability and the 5 forces all low to moderate, the next step in the 'outside in'-strategy-making process is to formulate a business strategy – how do you want to compete in your chosen industry? Strategic positioning is about positioning your firm within the industry where you can compete most effectively (see Figure 3.3). There are two generic choices available here. Either you can pursue a **Differentiation Strategy** or a **Cost Leadership Strategy** (see Porter, 2008b).

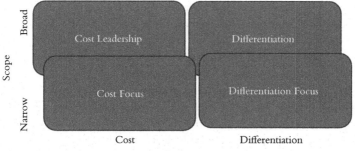

FIGURE 3.3 Generic strategies by Porter

A differentiation strategy is about differentiating your product or service offering(s) vis-à-vis your competitors. You compete on the basis of your differentiated product(s) or service(s) that vary across different customer demands. In the smartphone market Apple and Samsung handsets are differentiated from each other in terms of the design, operating system, applications, camera resolutions and other features. Apple and Samsung are both pursuing a differentiation strategy. Their strategies are 'generic' in the sense that they both compete on the same principle – offering differentiated products or services to their customers.

A cost leadership strategy is about striving to achieve the lowest cost structure in the industry. A firm that has achieved that objective can be said to be demonstrating cost leadership, but there may be others in the industry that are pursuing the same goal, but are not there yet. In the short-stay rental market, Airbnb has a cost leadership position. It has achieved this through its innovative business model which has allowed it to leverage spare room capacities that people have in their homes. It acts as a broker between the tourists and ordinary people who have spare rooms available.

Both cost leadership and differentiation strategies can be targeted at a broad market segment or a narrow one.

Problems with the linear view of strategy

The 'outside in' approach of strategy making starts with the industry analysis using the 5 forces and strategic groups, and concludes with the formulation of firm level strategies, such as Generic Strategies. Hence, it is a rather linear approach to strategy-making. It holds the view that an attractive industry is the source of superior profits for a firm. But the reality is that there are firms generating superior profitability in very unattractive industries. Take Dyson as an example. In the mid-1980s, the vacuum cleaner industry was in its mature stage, the purchasing decision was guided by the 'value for money' proposition. No one really thought that a manufacturing company of vacuum cleaners can command a huge premium in the market as the product design was standardized. If you had done a 5 forces analysis on the mid-1980s vacuum cleaner industry, your evaluation would have been that this is a deeply unattractive industry, with all the Forces scoring high. Then, Dyson made its entry into the market, and the structure of the market changed. Now there was a player that commanded a huge price premium, and, by virtue of its presence, created a new strategic group within the industry.

So, the 5 forces framework is a **static analysis**. It is a snapshot of the industry at a point in time. It tells you very little about how that industry structure came about, and how it is going to look in the future. It assumes an industry structure as a given. However, in reality, this is shaped by individual firm behaviour. Firms are not passive recipients of the industry structure; they shape it actively through their strategies.

The Generic Strategies are limited in their scope. If a firm strategy is mainly guided by its resources and capabilities, and not by an industry structure, then strategy is about exploiting its core resources and capabilities, the outcome of which may correspond to a differentiation or cost leadership strategy or a combination thereof. A hybrid strategy of cost leadership and differentiation is perfectly feasible if it is based on the core capabilities of the firm, but advocates of the 'outside in' approach explicitly warn against adopting a hybrid approach, suggesting that this may lead to the firm getting 'stuck in the middle'. [9]

Is Toyota 'stuck in the middle'? It has arguably excelled both in efficient production, such as Kaizen and the Just-in-Time Toyota Production System. The company offers differentiated products to its customers, for example the hybrid engine-based Toyota Prius or the upmarket Toyota Lexus range. You can claim that only if you are trying to artificially fit the reality to theory. A company is what a company does. Toyota started out as a low-cost producer of automobiles and has gradually acquired new capabilities which allowed to expand its product portfolio. This brings us to the main message of the book which is worth reiterating here: competitive success is rarely monocausal. The resources and capabilities that Toyota acquired in the 1980s and 1990s were mainly due to its extended 'reach' as it expanded internationally. Toyota also benefited from its 'roots' which are in Japan. The national environment affected Toyota's competitiveness in myriad ways. And, Toyota's 'recombination' capacity, its product and process innovations, were impacted by its resources, reach and roots (see, for example, Sturdevant, 2014).

Linking the 'inside out' and 'outside in' approach of strategy-making

The advocates of the two main schools of thought in strategy (see Figure 3.4) often take an adversarial position in relation to each other, arguing that their way is the right approach to strategy-making. This has a lot to do with the 'game of academic publishing', individual scholars trying to carve out their own distinctive identities within the field. In reality, there is a lot of common ground, and both positions have their merits and drawbacks.

Let's first acknowledge the obvious. There are industries that are structurally more profitable than others, and the industry structure is an emergent property

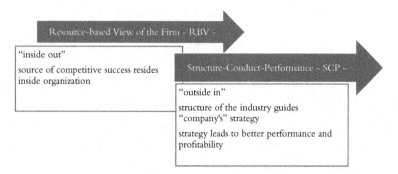

FIGURE 3.4 Comparing the 'inside out' and 'outside in' approach of strategy-making

of the strategic actions taken by players within the industry, each playing to its strengths. A differentiation strategy can be underpinned by R&D capabilities and a cost leadership strategy by manufacturing capabilities. The question of which comes first – the generic strategies or resources and capabilities – concerns only academics and not industry practitioners who have to get on with the job of competing and surviving in the industry. Linear strategy-making also almost never occurs in practice. So, the debate is a bit pointless. Competitive success is not about exercising a choice between attractive industries and unique resources and capabilities. These two are important pieces of the puzzle but they do not constitute the whole picture, as we will see in the next chapters.

CASE STUDY 3.1: DE BEERS DIAMONDS

Few items possess a stronger appeal to our imagination than diamonds. By their very essence, the value of diamonds is derived from their scarcity and their symbol of love, affection and commitment.

However, scarcity by itself does not provide the full picture of how diamonds emerged to become the very symbol of human love. Diamonds became a landmark symbol in almost any relationship, comprising engagement rings and jewellery given or acquired to celebrate personal moments of affection. The exclusivity of diamonds reinforces the uniqueness of human love.

One company was particularly successful in establishing itself as the landmark of how to market exclusivity and emotions to the global consumer market. Its name is De Beers Group,[1] a company with a revenue of US$4.6 billion in 2019,[2] which became close to a synonym of the diamond trade. It is no surprise that the 2019 annual industry report of De Beers bears the heading 'Diamonds and Love in the Modern World'.[3]

About half of all diamond jewellery given is an expression of love. However, even love appears to become subject to changes in societal preferences. Those expressions of love are often not related to marriage rituals alone but comprise a broad range of personal moments of cohabitation.

The roots of De Beers date back to the year 1888. It is only recently that the company's core activities of the exploration and mining of rough diamonds also comprise the marketing of polished diamonds and jewellery.

History

When in 1871 the brothers Diedrich Arnoldus and Johannes Nicolaas de Beer discovered diamonds on their family's farming ground in South Africa, the future prospects of their venture were yet beyond imagination. In 1888, the De Beers Consolidated Mines Limited was incorporated and Cecil Rhodes became the company's founding chairman.

During the tangles of the second Boer War in 1899 and the Great Depression during the 1930s which forced De Beers to close all its mines, one of the most pivotal steps to market diamonds to individual consumers took place in 1939, when De Beers initiated its own advertising campaign that led to the epochal slogan 'A diamond is forever' in 1947.

With this move, De Beers turned its historic business activities of exploration and mining into a new direction by directly marketing diamonds to the general consumer market. The company transformed itself from a mining and trading company in rough diamonds to an upmarket jewellery brand that became close to a synonym of diamonds in general. It appears that De Beers was able to come out stronger from the economic turmoil of the Great Depression and the Second World War. The company adapted to new and changing circumstances and identified areas for substantial profitability and sustaining growth.

Creating and losing a monopoly

De Beers was unusually successful in establishing a monopoly position in trading rough diamonds. One of the many marketing campaigns in the 1990s, for example, comprised broadcasting commercials that did not even display the company's name. A simple and aesthetic campaign displaying diamond jewellery together with De Beer's epochal slogan was considered sufficient to promote the company's interest.

Gaining a monopoly in a global industry sector is a major achievement for any firm; an achievement that displays strategic and commercial insights to integrate mining, trading and marketing activities into a coherent framework. However, keeping and sustaining such a hard-fought monopoly position became an even harder task. De Beers shows a recent decline in revenue after a peak in 2014 amounting to US$7.1 billion. In 2019, the number declined to US$4.6 billion. Within an industry sector that trades and markets natural resources, a strategy that emphasizes entry barriers against competitive forces is pivotal in sustaining a competitive advantage.

As such, De Beer's report separates the industry's value chain between downstream, midstream and upstream activities in both rough and polished diamonds. On the level of the global industry, the current developments of the diamond sector's value chain show a rather mixed picture of profitability and trends.

Downstream, the global consumer demand for polished diamonds increased by 1.9% in 2019, with one of the biggest market shares relating to the US with an annual demand of polished diamonds amounting to more than US$25 billion. Midstream, the trading activities declined in both rough and polished diamonds during 2018 and 2019. This was mainly due to a global decrease in liquidity and exchange rate fluctuations. Upstream, the value of the exploration and mining of rough diamonds increased slightly by around 1%.

The current position of De Beers could not differ more from its historical legacy.[4] In 1902, De Beers held a monopoly of about 90% of the global mining and marketing of rough diamonds. And conditions further improved. New countries joined the diamond mining industry and De Beers was able to acquire the exclusive trading rights. A 'single channel' strategy of mining, trading and marketing rough diamonds payed out handsomely to the Oppenheimer family, owning the majority of De Beers' share capital.

However, during the late 1990s, a number of countries that produced diamonds or hosted major trading hubs went against the dominant market force of De Beers. African countries, Israel, Canada, Australia and Russia formulated their own trading policies and opposed the 'single channel' strategy of De Beers. The monopoly position of the company deteriorated substantially.

The move forward

The forces of a stagnant global market demand amplified an increasing opposition from De Beers suppliers in rough diamonds. The company found a solution to those external forces to formulate a new business strategy to retail customers. In 2001, De Beers set up a new company, De Beers Diamond Jewellers.[5] Under this brand, De Beers produced and marketed self-branded jewellery for the global retail market. This jewellery was marketed through a chain of retail boutiques of which Old Bond Street, London became the first to open its doors in 2002. Its current network of jewellery boutiques comprises thirty shops and illustrates the long-term commitment of De Beers to establish a global network of retail boutiques.

Trends and developments of an industry of love and affection

The market for rough, polished and synthetic diamonds[6] experienced a number of changes recently and is strongly affected by general economic conditions. A loss in consumer confidence can therefore become a deterrent to De Beers' growth ambitions as much as any economic, social or political factor influencing global demand in diamonds and jewellery.

A number of annual industry reports outline a potential direction for the industry to develop. Industry research performed by Bain & Company, a consultancy firm, in 2018 gave their view on general sector trends in which 'a resilient industry shines through'.[7] The growth in rough diamond mining and a stable midstream profitability reflected improved prospects for the industry.

In 2019, MarketWatch expressed a similar positive opinion in their outlook to the year 2019–2025. Both production and profitability were expected to grow for the foreseeable future.[8] A view that was equally shared by McKinsey & Company in their 2014 report 'The jewellery industry in 2020'.[9]

> The trends that have unfolded in the apparel sector over the last three decades appear to be playing out in the jewellery sector, but at a much faster pace.

It remains to be seen how the industry of rough and polished diamonds will develop into the future, particularly after global economic conditions were affected by the outbreak of Covid-19. Practically all governments around the planet announced emergency aid programmes for faltering companies. The long-term effects of this global standstill and how this will resonate with consumer confidence will affect companies such as De Beers substantially. For sure, love will remain our most intimate human emotion. The only question is, how will De Beers respond to continue with marketing it?

Pointers to strategic conversations

1. Which of De Beers' portfolio of resources and capabilities led to competitive success?
2. How would you determine the unique resources and capabilities of De Beers?
3. Where is the value generated and captured in the diamond business?

McKinsey & Company, Industry Report, 2014

Sources

[1] **De Beers Group** company website: www.debeersgroup.com
[2] **Statista** – Revenue of De Beers from 2011 to 2019: www.statista.com/statistics/585681/revenue-of-de-beers/
[3] Company Report – The Diamond Insight Report 2019: www.debeersgroup.com/~/media/Files/D/De-Beers-Group/documents/reports/insights/the-diamond-insight-report-2019.pdf

[4] **Business Insider:** The incredible story of how De Beers created and lost the most powerful monopoly ever: www.businessinsider.com/history-of-de-beers-2011-12?international=true&r=US&IR=T

[5] **De Beers Jewellers** company website: www.debeers.com

[6] **Cape Town Diamond Museum** – What is the difference between real diamonds and synthetic diamonds? www.capetowndiamondmuseum.org/blog/2018/06/real-diamonds-vs-synthetic-diamonds/

[7] **Bain** Industry Report – The Global Diamond Industry 2018: www.bain.com/contentassets/a53a9fa8bf5247a3b7bb0b10561510c2/bain_diamond_report_2018.pdf

[8] **MarketWatch** – Diamonds and diamond jewelry market 2019 global industry demand, recent trends, size and share estimation by 2025 with top players: www.marketwatch.com/press-release/diamonds-and-diamond-jewelry-market-2019-global-industry-demand-recent-trends-size-and-share-estimation-by-2025-with-top-players---researchreportsworldcom-2019-11-27

[9] **McKinsey & Company** – A multifaceted future: The jewelry industry in 2020: www.mckinsey.com/industries/retail/our-insights/a-multifaceted-future-the-jewelry-industry-in-2020

CASE STUDY 3.2: MICROSOFT

Founded in 1975, Microsoft is the world's largest software company. It gained prominence for creating Windows, the first operating system that powered the rise of personal computing. Its journey since has been one of continual evolvement and reshaping of the business to meet computational technology needs, preferences and behaviours of the global technology consumers and enterprises in a rapidly digitalizing world.

A dynamic understanding of the rapid changes in the sector and the ability to remodel company skills and resources to adapt to those changes are critical to long-term sustainability of companies like Microsoft or Cisco in fast moving sectors like technology and telecommunications.

In the 1990s and early 2000s, Microsoft was the dominant player in the desktop and personal computer (PC) system software industry with the Windows operating system (OS) that powered these machines. Its Microsoft Office suite of productivity software was also a market leader. Two decades later, the Windows platform still retains 88% market share among all desktop OS's despite potent contenders like Google's Chrome OS and the ascendancy of open-source systems like Linux. Windows OS devices account for 35% of all web access despite the fact that less than 1% of all mobile devices globally run Windows OS (Google's Android and Apple's iOS have 99% market share between them).

This figure is important since the internet is the playground of the future, and more significant because there are 2 billion PCs globally compared to 1 billion tablets and 9 billion mobile phones (5 billion of which are smartphones, 2019 figures). The share of access to the web shows the strides and internal resource re-configurations that Microsoft is making to retain its classic competitive advantage of a PC OS maker in order to adapt, retain its prominence and gain future positional advantages in the new era technologies of Cloud, IOT (Internet of Things, for example internet embedded devices like smart meters) and 5G. In fact, Microsoft is already a formidable player in these new markets.

Microsoft Office: Transformation of legacy assets

Microsoft's Office productivity suite was the leading application for a prolonged period in the 1990s and early 2000s. The advent of Cloud-based computing, open source options like Open Office.org and potent rivals like G Suite from Google all collectively resulted in Microsoft losing its prominence in the following years.

But the company has since been slowly recapturing market share. Its realignment of internal resources and remodelling of the existing Office proposition to better exploit the new business opportunity of always-on, collaboration-seeking and connected consumer is a stellar example of dynamic capability development.

It did that by absorbing external changes that were occurring in the productivity tools software market, interpreted their impact, and then successfully reconfigured existing company assets into creating a future proof business model. The transformation was accelerated by a change in vision for the company by a new CEO in 2014.

Microsoft's resounding success for nearly three decades was largely driven by Windows which is a proprietary software that was sold on licence through OEM hardware manufacturers. Its Office packaged software was also a one-time licence revenue. It lacked web-enablement and online collaborative tools that its biggest competitor – Google's G Suite – had adopted early.

Under the new CEO, Microsoft sensed these new trends: Cloud-based document collaboration, off-line storage needs, cloud-based access and easy integration with other applications. It also took stock of its existing assets: compelling brand power, positive recall of both consumers and enterprise, and preference of users to buy familiar software as learning new software was a deterrent.

It seized the opportunity of the increasing need for collaboration and file sharing between employees in companies and adapted both its capabilities and its business model. It moved away from proprietary phone hardware and operating systems to an industry collaborative, cloud-first, mobile-first vision.

It changed from licences to a recurring monthly subscription, and cloud-enabled Microsoft Office. It became a collaborator of the open-source development community. It embraced adoption of the cloud, even turning into a vendor with its Azure intelligent cloud infrastructure services, challenging Amazon Web Services, the leading player. The brand presence of Windows and Office in large enterprises has proved an advantage in offering its new products and services.

The new Office 365 was launched on 28 June 2011, originally to enterprise users, and then in 2013 to the consumer with an enhanced customer support service. It quadrupled its market share to 35% in five years, and is being adopted at a faster pace than G Suite.

As a result, Microsoft's share price has multiplied six times between 2014 and 2020 to become the world's most valuable company, at $1.2 trillion (31 March 2020)[14] beating Apple, Amazon and Alphabet. In the last company results (January 2020), Office 365 Commercial revenue was reported to have grown at 27%, compared to the result of a year ago.[4]

Focus on 'Intelligent cloud'

Rapid advancement in new technologies such as Cloud, AI and 5G are not only reshaping how business is conducted, but also refashioning how people will live and work in the future. These technologies are expected to boost the size of the IT market from approximately $2.5 trillion today by an additional $2 trillion by the end of the decade.[9]

Of these, the adoption of 'Cloud' is gaining significance as it can provide 30–40% reduction in IT costs for companies. In fact, after a prolific rise in adoption in the last decade, 94% of all enterprises already use a cloud service, 30% of all IT budgets are allocated to Cloud and 50% of enterprises spend more than $1.2m annually on Cloud services.[12]

Microsoft sensed and seized this opportunity. The advent of the new CEO in 2014 accelerated its activity in this area. It tasked itself to transform from a PC software licence company to becoming an indispensable partner to help clients compete, grow and create new value, with the cloud being a core proposition.

Its approach has been innovative – focusing on helping to transform its client's business, rather than just being a pure infrastructure or storage cloud platform provider like most others offering 'platform as a service', a market that is gradually commoditizing to a diminishing value price-play.

Microsoft's 'Azure' Cloud platform differentiates itself as an 'intelligent cloud' that caters to the entire 'IT Estate' of its customers, or in other words, is a cloud-enabling business solutions provider. Azure is built on the three tenets of 'global', trusted' and 'hybrid' that delivers all components of cloud and edge computing in a consistent and comprehensive approach.

One of Microsoft's biggest assets is its substantive legacy from the last three decades of being a global leader. That asset is a customer base of Fortune 500 organizations, global companies, small businesses, startups and technology sector participants. For example, its customers include 85% of the world's banks which typically have a higher compliance and data security requirement than other sectors. Microsoft extended its existing capabilities with Azure, rapidly enlarging its reach to 34 global regions that was nearly twice the reach of Amazon. It also obtained 47 compliance certifications and attestations, a critical need for the banking industry, and became the world's most compliant hyper-scale cloud.

It also used its standing to build partnerships with other industry players like Oracle, championing inter-operability in the cloud market.

Amazon Web Services (AWS) was the early leader among cloud providers, and still commands nearly half of all cloud services market share at 47.8%, more than three times that of Microsoft's at 15.5%.[1] However, Microsoft's intelligent cloud is growing rapidly, achieving between 60 and 70% revenue growth in the last few quarters while Amazon's growth slowed to a humbler 34% in a comparable timeframe, having peaked at 81% growth rate in 2015.

Collaborations and strategic partnerships

Collaborations and partnerships are a source of knowledge that can help firms to benchmark their internal practices and prevent strategic blind spots. Fast-changing markets require the ability to reconfigure the firm's asset structure and accomplish the necessary internal and external transformations, but engineering change can be expensive and time-consuming. Alliances and acquisitions are a nimble alternative to bring the needed new strategic assets into the firm.

The capability to forge alliances and identify acquisitions implies the abilities to sense the environment, evaluate options and then reconfigure processes to remain ahead of the competition.

Microsoft has been savvy in forging partnerships from its early days. Its few first strategic alliances with Intel and IBM to supply OS to personal computers were the key to its success in creating a global brand. It has redoubled on that philosophy of 'Putting Partners First' with its One Commercial Partner programme and 'One accelerant', its intellectual property co-sell programme.

Microsoft's partner ecosystem generates 95% of its commercial revenue; it encourages innovation and generated $8 billion in revenues since these programmes began in July 2017.

Microsoft also actively engages in co-specialization with other companies and leaders in other industries to jointly develop intellectual property and other assets that add to its dynamic capabilities. These combined specialisms are usually more valuable than those developed individually, and often create competitive advantage for Microsoft's products and services in different sectors.

New business model: Client-first, not profit-first

The design and performance of a company's business model is an integral input to maintain the vitality of a company's dynamic capabilities. Microsoft has been able to transform its business model not just to address changes in its environment, but also as a leader in bringing change to the technology industry.

Microsoft's recent business model reflects this sharp customer-centric focus and is proving to be a determinant in its competitive advantage. Two examples of this follow:

a. In a radical departure from salesperson compensation and incentives being based on quantum of sales, it is now linked to actual customers' use of the product or service and the value that is derived by the customer of the solution.
b. Embracing a customer as a commercial digital and technology partner by taking on their digital assets, improving them and then jointly selling them to other industry players. Recent examples of this are Boeing, AT&T and NTT, as portrayed by the press coverage shown below.

This strategy allows integration of collaborative knowledge and technology capacities of its partners. These integrative external activities resemble open innovation mechanisms that companies are increasingly adopting to overcome the limited efficiency of closed in-house R&D in the technology sector where products have a short life cycle.

> 'Boeing is working together with Microsoft, a leader in the technology space, to bring innovative operational efficiency solutions to global aviation customers', explains Andrew Gendreau, the director of advanced information solutions in Boeing's Digital Aviation division. 'Boeing brings in their deep subject matter expertise, complimented by Microsoft's deep technical expertise, and together we'll be bringing new, innovative customer solutions to market'[16] (18 July 2016)
>
> Multiyear collaboration will accelerate AT&T's 'public cloud first' internal transformation and deliver new customer offerings built on AT&T's network and Microsoft's cloud[17] (17 July 2019)
>
> Microsoft has struck up yet another partnership. On Tuesday it has inked a multiyear alliance with industry heavyweight NTT. The alliance merges NTT's ICT infrastructure, managed services and cybersecurity expertise with Microsoft's cloud platform and AI technologies to enable new digital solutions to help enterprise customers everywhere accelerate their digital transformation.[6] (10 December 2019)

Learning from failures in hardware devices

Windows OS was a pathbreaker product. Microsoft's agreement with IBM to supply the lifeblood MS-DOS for the latter's personal computers was not only the key to Microsoft's future, it changed the course of the PC industry. Strategic partnerships as a journey to developing dynamic capabilities, either organically or inorganically, does not always go right. As an example, here is an article from 2011:

> Nokia and Microsoft were hoping two wrongs make a right
> 'Nokia and Microsoft are to join forces in a bid to topple Apple and Google in the mobile phone market. The two firms today announced a "broad strategic partnership" that will see Nokia phones running Microsoft software'.

In the late 2000s, the usage of mobile devices was gaining ground. The launch of Apple's iPhone and Google's Android, both in 2007, spurred a smartphone revolution. Over the next few years, their biggest victim would be Nokia.

Microsoft too had a problem with its core Windows business. Open source software, non-PC access to the rapidly growing internet and high licence fees for its software were all flatlining its growth.

A partnership between two failed 'mobile strategies' to catch up with Apple and Google in the mobile device market seemed like an attractive joint venture that could leverage complementary capabilities, global reach, brand equity and scale. Microsoft's core capability of its Windows mobile OS would complement Nokia's hardware proficiencies and a mobile market share of 41%. The combined assets would drive innovation in both to together create a global mobile ecosystem.

The journey to enhanced capabilities and success in the mobile device market, however, did not fructify. Nokia was unable to compete against the tide of Android manufacturers, most prominent of which was Samsung. Windows Phone 7 turned in a lacklustre performance, too, as a desktop OS attempting to adapt to touch-driven highly interactive smartphone interfaces. Microsoft acquired Nokia in 2013, just before CEO Steve Ballmer stepped down. It wrote off nearly $7.6 billion in the final quarter of 2015.

At its core, Microsoft is not a hardware company, but its Surface line-up of two-in-ones, initially launched in 2012, have been gradually gaining franchise. It has now dramatically improved its hardware capabilities, and is launching its first ever dual-screen mobile computer in 2020. The Surface Neo folds up like a book and could finally cement Microsoft's position in the hardware arena.

Pointers to strategic conversations

1. How has Microsoft been able to reconfigure its resources and capabilities over the years?
2. Which organizational processes allowed Microsoft to 'sense' the changes in the business environment? Which organizational processes allowed it to 'seize' the opportunities?
3. How critical has 'open innovation' been to Microsoft's success?
4. Can we say that Microsoft demonstrates 'dynamic capabilities'?

Sources

[1] How #1 Microsoft is beating Amazon, Google and everyone else in The Cloud: The strategic breakdown: Bob Evans, Forbes.com, 17 September 2018.

[2] From 'Evil empire' to Model citizen? How Microsoft's good deeds work to its competitive advantage, by Lisa Stiffler, Geekwire on 7 March 2019, Contributions by Monica Nickelsburg.

[3] Microsoft's next Act: April 2018 | Podcast – McKinsey Quarterly.

[4] Wikipedia: List of public corporations by market capitalization.

[5] Microsoft website: https://azure.microsoft.com/en-gb/blog/cloud-innovations-empowering-it-for-business-transformation/

[6] Microsoft website blogs: https://blogs.microsoft.com/transform/2016/07/18/boeing-and-microsoft-taking-the-next-step-together-in-digital-aviation/

[7] Microsoft website: News, 17 July 2019, AT&T and Microsoft announce a strategic alliance to deliver innovation with cloud, AI and 5G https://news.microsoft.com/2019/07/17/att-and-microsoft-announce-a-strategic-alliance-to-deliver-innovation-with-cloud-ai-and-5g/

[8] Fierce Telecom website announcement: 10 December 2019: www.fiercetelecom.com/telecom/microsoft-strikes-up-another-strategic-alliance-time-ntt

[9] Nokia and Microsoft Strategic Alliance, 16 May 2017, original article appeared in PCWorld.

[10] Inspired and powered by partners: https://blogs.microsoft.com/blog/2019/02/05/inspired-and-powered-by-partners/

[11] Cloud adoption statistics for 2020: HostingTribunal.com.

[12] Gartner.com: Cloud services Magic Quadrant 2019.

[13] Garvin, D.A. (1988) *Managing quality: The strategic and competitive edge.* New York: The Free Press.

[14] Amit, R. and Schoemaker, P.J.H. (1993). Strategic assets and organizational rent. *Strategic Management Journal* 14(1).

[15] Techcrunch.com: 29 January 2020, Microsoft shares rise after it beats revenue, profit expectations, Azure posts 62% growth https://techcrunch.com/2020/01/29/microsoft-shares-rise-after-it-beats-revenue-profit-expectations-azure-posts-62-growth/

[16] April 2015 SEC filing.

[17] https://thenextweb.com/offers/2020/05/16/seo-matters-this-package-of-web-analysis-tools-can-hlp-reshape-your-web-performance/

Conclusion

Resources and capabilities of the organization are an important ingredient in the recipe mix that ultimately delivers competitive success in the marketplace. In this chapter, we have developed an understanding of resources and capabilities: the distinction between the two, the different kinds of organizational resources, and how to identify your key resources and capabilities. We have also discussed their transient nature: what delivers competitive advantage today may not do so tomorrow. We showed how the dynamic capabilities of the firm allow reconfiguration of resources, recharging their productive capacity within the changed context. We discussed the idea of strategic positioning and contrasted it with the resource-based view of the firm.

Notes

1 The idea of capabilities is closely linked with the notion of organizational routines. See Winter, 2000. Also see Zollo and Winter, 1999: 38.
2 For a good introduction to the idea, see Barney, 1991.
3 Apple for example has consistently outperformed its rivals in the smartphone sector in terms of profitability on a sustained basis. This demonstrates competitive advantage. An analysis of Apple's profitability vs. competitors can be found at this link: www.forbes.com/ sites/chuckjones/2018/03/02/apple-continues-to-dominate-the-smartphone-profit-pool/#77c001dc61bb.
4 The RBV framework has been critiqued by some for being tautological. Resources and capabilities are deemed to be valuable because they have been found to be valuable (competitive success). This circular reasoning makes the process of generation of competitive advantage akin to a black box. The idea of causal ambiguity, a core tenet of RBV, underlines this point. For a more detailed critique, see Priem and Butler, 2001.
5 Dynamic capabilities advocates clearly see the idea as a response to RBV, filling some of the gaps in the latter. See Collis, 1994.
6 For a good overview of the idea of dynamic capabilities, see Teece et al., 1997.
7 A good example is Nokia in the mobile handset market. Its market leadership position quickly disappeared with the advent of smartphones. How about Kodak in the camera market? For them, the killer technology was the digital SLR. The irony is that Kodak was the first to develop the digital camera yet failed to capitalize on it.
8 For a historical overview of the SCP Paradigm, see Bianchi, 2013.
9 See Porter (1985). Porter advocates against being 'stuck in the middle', arguing that it is an unsustainable position, particularly in matured industries.

Further reading

Barney, J. (1991). Firm resources and sustained competitive advantage. *Journal of management*, *17*(1), 99–120.
Barney, J. B. (1995). Looking inside for competitive advantage. *Academy of management perspectives*, *9*(4), 49–61.
Bianchi, P. (2013). Bain and the origins of industrial economics. *European review of industrial economics and policy*, 7.
Caves, R. E., & Porter, M. E. (1977). From entry barriers to mobility barriers: Conjectural decisions and contrived deterrence to new competition. *The quarterly journal of economics*, *91*(2), 241–261.
Chamberlin, E. (1962). *The theory of monopolistic competition*. Cambridge, MA: Harvard University Press.

Collis, D. J. (1994). Research note: how valuable are organizational capabilities? *Strategic management journal*, *15*(S1), 143–152.

Ferguson, P. R., & Ferguson, G. J. (1994). The structure-conduct-performance paradigm. In *Industrial economics* (pp. 13–37). London: Palgrave.

Porter, M. E. (1985). *Competitive advantage: Creating and sustaining superior performance*. New York: Free Press.

Porter, M. E. (2008a). *Competitive strategy: Techniques for analyzing industries and competitors*. New York: Simon and Schuster.

Porter, M. E. (2008b). The five competitive forces that shape strategy. *Harvard business review*, *86*(1), 25–40.

Priem, R. L., & Butler, J. E. (2001). Is the resource-based 'view' a useful perspective for strategic management research? *Academy of management review*, *26*(1), 22–40.

Robinson, J. (1933). *The economics of imperfect competition*. London: Macmillan.

Sturdevant, D. (2014). (Still) learning from Toyota. *McKinsey quarterly*, 1 February. www.mckinsey.com/industries/automotive-and-assembly/our-insights/still-learning-from-toyota

Teece, D. J., Pisano, G., & Shuen, A. (1997). Dynamic capabilities and strategic management. *Strategic management journal*, *18*(7), 509–533.

Winter, S. G. (2000). The satisficing principle in capability learning. *Strategic management journal*, *21*(10–11), 981–996.

Zollo, M., & Winter, S. G. (1999). *From organizational routines to dynamic capabilities*. Fontainebleau, France: INSEAD.

4

RECOMBINATION

The process of innovation

Innovation is recombination.[1] It is the process through which existing ideas, resources and capabilities are recombined in new ways. When Isaac Newton, founder of classical mechanics, said, 'If I have seen further it is by standing on the shoulders of Giants', he was reiterating an important principle of innovation – that it is cumulative. When Albert Einstein said 'combinatory play seems to be the essential feature in productive thought' he was articulating another – that innovation is inherently re-combinatorial: the mixing of existing ideas to produce something new. This chapter is about innovation, focusing on its central process – recombination. To present a rounded perspective, we have not only synthesized conventional theories, but also borrowed freely from hitherto neglected disciplines like evolutionary anthropology to enhance our understanding of innovation and creativity.

Understanding innovation: Different perspectives

Innovation can be looked at from different perspective. You can try to understand why some people are more creative than others, why some industries innovate more than others, why some firms excel in bringing out new products, why some physical locations such as cities, nations or particular regions, are good in fostering creativity. Each perspective is important and, moreover, we argue, they are interlinked. It is, after all, not an accident that creative people and firms cluster together in specific physical locations (often cities, sometimes regions). Lots of technologically innovative firms have congregated in Silicon Valley. Similarly, many organizations and people involved in creative arts are in London. The link between the place and the intensity of innovation is empirically well-established.

Innovation at the macro level: City, region and nation

Are some countries more innovative than others? It depends on what you think innovation is. If innovation is measured in terms of patents and other formal intellectual properties, then certainly some countries are ahead of others (see Figure 4.1).

But patents are an imperfect measure of innovation. After all, not all patents translate into new products or services. Evolutionary anthropologists hold that being innovative is second nature to humans. We cannot help being innovative, provided the conditions are right.[2] So, it makes sense to focus on the conditions that may differ across national boundaries.

National innovation system and triple helix thesis

As discussed in Chapter 2, globalization and nation-states are two ideas integrally linked together; global flows are those movements in goods, services, labour, capital and ideas that flow across national frontiers. The way these flows circulate within the national boundaries depend on national institutions. Institutions are 'rules of the game'[3]. They can be formal as well as informal. Formal institutions are the rule of law, property rights, policies governing interactions between the government, industry and academia. Informal institutions or norms are the ways of behaviour, non-codified practices prevalent within the nation-state. One of the reasons innovative capacity of nations differ from each other is because the institutional environment is different in each country. The innovation process (see Figure 4.2) is sometimes conceptualized in the following way:

The above can be reframed as:

Basic research => Applied research => Commercialization => Usage

The idea being that basic research is carried out for its own sake, without any consideration of practical applications; applied research on the other hand is focused on providing solutions to real life problems; commercialization takes the process further by converting ideas into commercial products and services, which are then consumed by the end-users.

In many countries, policymakers subscribe to this system-view of innovation. Within this innovation system, government funds almost all basic research and some applied research. Private corporations engage in some applied research and play the dominant role in the commercialization process and subsequent interactions with end-users.[4] The system view of innovation or what is more commonly known as the National Innovation System (NIS)[5] became popular with policymakers around mid-twentieth century.[6] The two World Wars alerted national governments to the importance of basic and applied research which may lead to improved military technologies. This view further gained strength during the Cold War which saw an arms race between the United States and the erstwhile Soviet Union. The 1960s and 1970s saw large-scale funding of basic and applied research by government.[7]

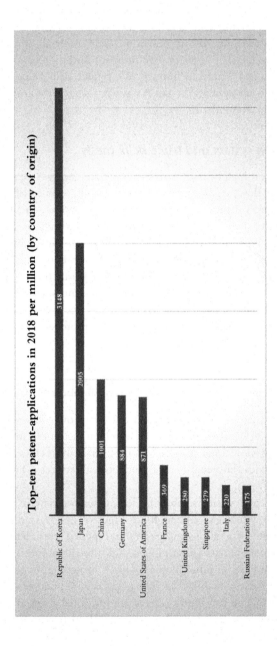

FIGURE 4.1 Patents per country

Source: WIPO statistics database. Last updated: April 2020

FIGURE 4.2 Invention – innovation – usage

Universities increasingly became the favourite vehicle for conducting research, and consequently, autonomous research institutes fell out of favour.

The 1980s saw a pushback against the prevalent orthodoxy which held that commercialization of university research can be carried out only by the private sector (see Figure 4.3). With the enactment of the Bayh-Dole Act in the United States, universities were able to exploit fully the intellectual properties generated out of government sponsored research. Spinouts and licensing of technologies by universities became more common, academia started to become more involved in the commercialization of their own intellectual properties. The system perspective on innovation evolved likewise. Conceptual frameworks such as mode 2 knowledge production[8] and the triple helix thesis[9] emphasize the need for universities to be more entrepreneurial. Mode 2 Knowledge advocates highlight the need for academia to engage in research that is useful and context driven. They urge academics to venture out from their ivory towers, investigate real societal problems and provide solutions thereof. The triple helix thesis, which builds on NIS and mode 2 knowledge production, argues that universities need to be more proactive in the commercialization process of the original knowledge that they produce. The most favoured vehicle for this is of course university spinouts. Academic entrepreneurship (measured in number of spinouts) is most prevalent in old established universities such as Oxford and Cambridge in the UK.[10] This also emphasizes the importance of location. Successful academic entrepreneurship thrives within science clusters, embedded in specific locations.[11]

Creative cities and clusters

Cities, more than nations, are the innovation hotspots of the world. In the UK, London stands out as the innovation hotspot; in India it is Bangalore. The innovation capacity of the nation is not evenly distributed across the landscape; it is concentrated in specific locations and most of these clusters are cities. Location is a key ingredient in the competitive success mix. We have devoted more attention to this relevant aspect and how it affects the growth of companies in Chapter 6, Roots: Power of the place. Cities like London and Bangalore are creative primarily because of their diversity, both populational and occupational. Why is diversity important? Mainly because it facilitates the recombination process. New ideas, products, processes and services emerge almost spontaneously when people from different aspects of life congregate in a relatively small physical space. Cities are

- Mode 2 Knowledge Production -

- Triple Helix Model -

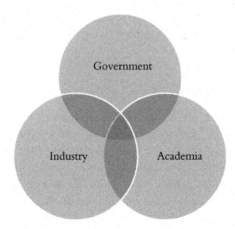

FIGURE 4.3 Comparison of mode 2 knowledge production and the triple helix thesis

cradles of civilization, and they are so because they are particularly adept at fostering innovation.[12]

From the firm perspective, a key strategic decision is about its location, where it is based. Co-locating with similar firms in a cluster brings about multiple benefits.

Innovation at the industry level

Some industries are more innovative than others. For example, the pace of technological change is faster in the smartphone industry compared with the oil industry. The Technology S Curve helps us to understand the dynamics of technological change within an industry.

Innovation at the component and architectural levels

Technological innovations can happen at both component and architectural levels.[13] These innovations can be incremental or radical in nature. Let's develop our understanding of these commonly used innovation concepts – component, architectural, incremental and radical – by turn (see Figure 4.4).

Consider the personal computer. It has **components** (screen, a central processing unit (CPU), a random-access memory (RAM), keyboard, software, etc.) and it has an overall **architecture**, the way these components interact with each other to deliver the functions that make the PC a useful product to us. The sustained improvements in performance of the components like CPU, RAM, operating system and screen are **incremental innovations**. When the technology of the component itself changes we call it **modular innovation**. For example, the technology of the PC screen has changed over time from the cathode ray tube to LCDs. This transformation is a modular innovation. When there is a fundamental change in the way these components interact with each other, we call it **architectural innovation.** A smartphone and a PC perform quite a few similar functions, yet the architecture of the smartphone is vastly different from that of the PC. The smartphone is an architectural innovation. **Radical innovation** brings about

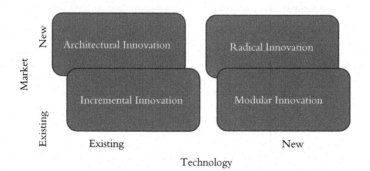

FIGURE 4.4 Innovation: incremental, modular, architectural and radical

transformation both at the component and architectural level. Coming back to the example of the smartphone, it was radical in the sense that both the components, like a device's memory, battery and screen, and the architecture were changed fundamentally. And this brings us to an important point, namely that there exists considerable interplay between these different forms of innovation. Innovations at the component level may trigger innovations at the architectural level, and this pattern can be observed in the smartphone case.

The Technology S Curve

There is a general pattern of technological change in a given industry. Improvements in **product performance** are slow in the initial stages, then there is a period of sustained improvements, but ultimately technological advancements taper off (see Figure 4.5).

New products that are introduced in the industry often start at a lower performance level than existing products. But these new products also improve with time and they can and do surpass the performance level of the older products (see Figure 4.6).

It is important to recognize here that the nature of innovation changes during the different stages of the **product life cycle (PLC)**.[14] The product life cycle is sometimes referred to as the **industry life cycle**. We will use these terms interchangeably, as synonyms. Products, typically, undergo four main stages of evolution – birth, growth, mature and decline (see Figure 4.7).

The duration of each of these stages differs significantly across different industries, and not all products experience this pattern.[15] Nevertheless, there is enough empirical data out there to say that the industry or product life cycle pattern is found in many industries, particularly those that are technology intensive.

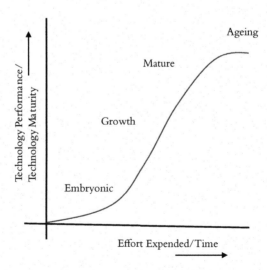

FIGURE 4.5 The Technology S Curve

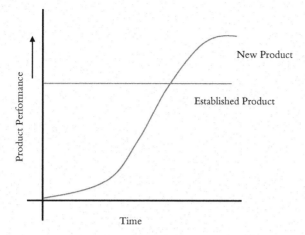

FIGURE 4.6 Product performance: new vs. established

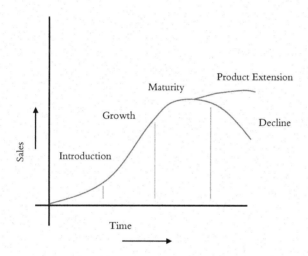

FIGURE 4.7 Product life cycle

So, what leads to a distinctive pattern? After all, products are not biological organisms. The term 'life cycle' may be a bit misleading. It may suggest that there is something universal about this pattern. It is worth reiterating here that PLC is a common but not a universal pattern. The common pattern arises because similar dynamics are at play within many industries.

At the initial stages of a new industry, there are many product designs competing against each other to become the **Dominant Design** of the industry.

Dominant design

At the birth of an industry, alternative technologies compete against each other to become the industry standard.[16] Think of the automobile industry at its infancy in the late nineteenth and early twentieth century. At that stage, there were several alternative technologies to propel the carriage: steam, electric and of course the internal combustion engine. For quite some time, it was not clear which technology would be the eventual winner. And then came Model T of the Ford Motor Company which was based on the internal combustion engine, and it made that technology the dominant design for the automotive industry.

Once the dominant design is established, the performance parameters become clear to the manufacturers and they can invest in mass production which in turn brings down the unit cost of the product leading to higher consumption and this kickstarts the growth phase of the industry – representing the steep upward sloping curve of the PLC. Performance of the product continuously improves throughout the growth phase through incremental innovations. Eventually, this stops, and the industry enters the mature phase, where product innovations taper off, the demand is saturated, but process innovations continue that make production more efficient.

The last stage is the decline. Why does the demand decline for the product? Because consumers migrate to a new technology. The new technology typically makes an entry to the industry when the incumbent is at the growth or mature stage of the PLC. Following the S Curve pattern discussed earlier, the performance level of the new technology often starts at a lower level than the existing one, and there is a competition for a new dominant design, but when that is resolved, the performance improves rapidly, which triggers the shifting of consumer allegiance to the new product and consequently the decline of the older product. So, the disruption of the established product by a new entrant is the main cause of the decline phase of PLC.

Disruptive innovation

Disruptions can happen both at the component and architectural levels (see Figure 4.8). It has been found that while the incumbents are quite adept at making

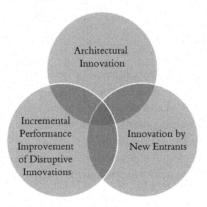

FIGURE 4.8 Key features of disruptive innovation

new innovations at the component level, the new entrants are better at this at the architectural level.[17] Upending of the incumbents at the architectural level has been defined as disruptive innovation.

A popular example of disruptive innovation is the disruption of large integrated steel works by mini mills. Traditionally most of the world's steel has been produced by large integrated steel mills which convert iron ore into steel bars by running 24/7 blast furnaces. Mini mills, in contrast, reuse scrap steel to make steel bars. The cost of running a mini mill is significantly lower than that of an integrated steel mill. Initially, for the integrated steel mills the cost disadvantage was not a problem. They were able to produce high quality steel bars that commanded a price premium. They were happy to let mini mills take the lower end of the market that dealt in low grade steel with low prices. But over time, the mini mills improved their production process and were able to produce high quality steel while retaining their cost advantage over integrated steel mills. It is then that mini mills became a disruptive innovation for the incumbents. The architecture of the production process of the mini mills is fundamentally different from that of the large integrated mills. The mini mill owners were typically new entrants into the industry.

The key features of disruptive innovation are:

a. Typically, the innovation is at the architectural level
b. Generally, the innovation is brought about by new entrants to the industry
c. Normally, the performance of the disruptive innovation starts at a lower level than the incumbent's product and improves rapidly over time

Innovation at the firm level

There are different kinds of innovation. Ryanair innovates by having a 25 minute turnaround time[18] of their aircraft. Apple innovates by producing ergonomically designed products. Oxford Brookes University (where one of the authors works as a lecturer) innovates by delivering a blended learning MBA targeting busy executives. Netflix innovates by transforming the business model of the television industry.

Firms are usually good in one specific form of innovation. Very rarely comes along a company like Toyota that has excelled in different kinds of innovation. The Toyota Production System (TPS) is a very different kind of innovation from the hybrid engine on which the Toyota Prius is based, yet the company has been successful in both. However, it is the exception that proves the rule. Different forms of innovation required different sets of resources and capabilities. Product innovation typically requires R&D capability and resources. Process innovation requires engineers who are capable of optimizing production activities. It is difficult for a particular organization to have these very different sets of capabilities in-house and ensure that they are of the highest quality. Specialization is a key feature of the modern capitalist economy, and this trend is prevalent within the innovation domain as well.

The incremental-radical continuum

The term radical innovation is loosely bandied about in management literature. Tiny product or process improvements and recycled old ideas are given the 'radical' label. Historians of technology have correctly surmised that from a technological standpoint, most innovations are incremental in nature.[19] Even the internet, which is a genuine 'radical innovation', would not be made possible without earlier innovations such as the computer, and network technologies like 'packet switching'. Radical innovation can be conceptualized on two dimensions – technological and meaning. The railways were an incremental innovation in terms of technology. The components of railways – the steam engine, the track, the carriage – were already there; the genius of railway pioneers was to recombine them in a new configuration. However, the radicalness of the innovation is in the way it transformed society. Railways meant that people could suddenly travel to distant places in hours which earlier used to take days. Not only did it accelerate the Industrial Revolution in Britain, the railways transformed lives of ordinary people in numerous ways. Most radical innovations are therefore 'radical' in their meaning to us and not necessarily in terms of their underlying technologies (see Figure 4.9).

Alternative innovation approaches: Open vs. closed

From the late nineteenth century onward, the for-profit private firm, through in-house R&D, became the dominant force in the generation of product innovations. This kickstarted the closed model of innovation which yet remains the preferred approach of the corporate world, though with notable exceptions. In the closed model of innovation, organizations are focused on protecting intellectual properties that may or may not have been generated through their own efforts. The model is predicated on exploitation of privately held intellectual properties like patents, utility models and copyrights.[20]

The open model of innovation, in contrast, puts the emphasis on collaboration with external stakeholders. Wikipedia is a great example of the open model of innovation. This internet encyclopedia is entirely organized through a community

FIGURE 4.9 The incremental–radical continuum

of volunteers. Anyone can post information on Wikipedia which then gets checked/ moderated/updated/removed by others. This open approach has proved quite robust, and arguably the rise of Wikipedia directly led to the demise of the printed version of Encyclopædia Britannica, which pursued a more closed approach (strong editorial direction, full-time paid contributors, etc.).

The popularity of the term 'Open Innovation' has been coterminous with the explosion of information and communication technologies thereby giving the impression that this approach is of relatively recent origin[21]. However, innovation has always flourished through open collaborations, and it is the closed model, with its focus on appropriating what is often public knowledge, that is the break from the norm.

The main argument for a closed-innovation approach is that strong protection of intellectual properties encourages more innovation. The closed model of innovation, arguably brings about greater focus, shortening the time required for an idea to be transformed into an actual product. Apple traditionally has pursued a closed approach to innovation, basing its computers, laptops and smartphones on proprietary operating systems rather than using available industry standards that are more open in nature.

The open approach to innovation is messier for sure. But it has the potential to generate more ideas. **User-led innovation** is one of the many manifestations of the open approach.[22] Take the example of mountain bikes. Early forms of mountain bikes were not produced in the R&D labs of bicycle companies. Rather, cyclists who were keen to conquer the mountain terrains modified standard bikes (with heavier shock absorbers, for example). They were the lead-users who showed the way to the bicycle manufacturers who gratefully capitalized on this open innovation and came up with their mountain bike range. They converted public knowledge to private property.

Open Source Innovation is a specific reaction to this appropriation of public knowledge for private gain. It is a reaction against the pervasive use of intellectual property rights like patents and copyrights by big corporations particularly in the software segment. By freely sharing software codes, proponents of open source software believed that the pace of innovation will quicken as it is based on the collective wisdom of experts. In many instances, this assumption has been proven correct. Successful open source software projects include GIMP (image manipulation), VLC media player, Audacity (an audio editor), Firefox (a web-browser) and others.

Overall, the open approach to innovation puts greater emphasis on collaboration with external actors. The contentious issue is the ownership of intellectual properties that are generated through such collaborations. Some commentators and scholars encourage private appropriation of intellectual properties that are generated through the open approach. Indeed, they emphasize that this is the way to generate superior profits, as open innovation, if done right, has the potential to significantly lower the cost of R&D. Others highlight the ethics of this strategy.

Innovation at the individual level

The discussion on innovation in standard management texts is usually kept at the firm and industry levels. Sometimes, the national or regional level is also included. But you will be hard pressed to find strategy texts that explore this at the level of the individual. To be clear, there are plenty of books that explore individual creativity, but they are not strategic management texts, and they do not scale up their exploration to organizational, industry and regional levels. Moreover, these treatises typically treat creativity as an elusive elixir that few have access to. The suggestion usually is that there are extraordinarily creative people out there who are just born that way. In other words, there is disconnect between the macro and micro level explanations of innovation within the literature.

We follow a different route here for two reasons. First, we believe that creativity and innovation is a human condition. Humans have been creative right from the inception of our species. This view is informed by the rich literature on human creativity within the anthropological literature in general and, in particular, the evolutionary anthropology stream. Second, we believe in creative unity. The dynamics of innovation and creativity are actually similar across different domains. One may think that creativity in art, science and technology involve different processes but it has been shown that in reality a creativity unity exists among these different fields.[23] Similarly, there is unity between the different levels – macro (regions and nations), meso (the industry or firm) and micro the (individual). What explains innovation at the level of the individual should not, at the least, contradict the explanations provided at more meso and macro levels.

Quite a lot of the innovation literature is cultish. What do we mean by this? Simply that it bows its head to the Cult of the Individual. The inventor or innovator is regarded as a superior being, different to us, mere mortals. Like magicians, they conjure up new products and services out of thin air. The focus is on the individual, partly because the process through which innovation actually happens is complex and, quite often, opaque. Encountering blind alleys and vaguely aware of our blind spots, we take the easy way out – we characterize innovation as a black box and suggest that only a select few, the fabled inventors, have the key to open it. The popular business literature is particularly adept at mythologizing the 'entrepreneur or inventor as a superior being' narrative.

Who discovered fire? Who figured out that a sharpened wooden stick makes hunting more effective? Who invented agriculture? We do not know these 'inventors', yet these innovations fundamentally changed our lives. What is clear is that innovating is a human condition, we have innovated as long as we have existed. So, it stands to reason that anthropology can shed some light on how new ideas become accepted and entrenched in human societies. Anthropologists are empirically minded – they observe human interactions in real time, often in traditional societies, and draw insights from those observations. Business studies, in contrast, has long been in thrall to economics which excels in abstract thinking and is often divorced from empirical realities. Business studies, by and large, has ignored anthropology. This is unfortunate as we think we can draw lots of insights from this empirically driven discipline with its focus firmly on real human interactions.

So, what light can anthropology shine on innovation? Consider the following excerpt from a paper written by two evolutionary anthropologists:[24]

> (I)nnovations, large or small, do not require heroic geniuses any more than your thoughts hinge on a particular neuron. Rather, just as thoughts are an emergent property of neurons firing in our neural networks, innovations arise as an emergent consequence of our species' psychology applied within our societies and social networks. Our societies and social networks act as collective brains. Individuals connected in collective brains, selectively transmitting and learning information, often well outside their conscious awareness, can produce complex designs without the need for a designer—just as natural selection does in genetic evolution. The processes of cumulative cultural evolution result in technologies and techniques that no single individual could recreate in their lifetime, and do not require its beneficiaries to understand how and why they work.

This argument turns on its head the conventional wisdom on innovation. Instead of focusing on the mystic qualities of entrepreneur/inventor/innovator, the suggestion here is that our evolved brains are adapted for social learning, and when that is applied within a social context, innovation is inevitable. Moreover, innovations are not necessarily 'designed' and can occur through fortuitous accidents or errors in copying. The paper gives some great examples of unintended innovations.

> (T)he number of major inventions and discoveries owing to accidents is impressive. These include Teflon, Velcro, X-rays, penicillin, safety glass, microwave ovens, Post-It notes, vulcanized rubber, polyethylene and artificial sweeteners. The classic serendipitous discovery was Alexander Fleming, who discovered penicillin after noting that his colonies of staphylococci had been killed by a mould that had drifted in through an open window. Unlike his discovery, Fleming's mode of discovery was neither remarkable, nor unusual. The basis for microwave ovens was discovered when Percy Spencer noted that radar microwaves had melted a chocolate bar in his pocket. The hard, vulcanized, rubber in tyres was discovered when Charles Goodyear accidentally brought rubber into contact with a hot stove and noted that instead of melting, it produced a more robust rubber. The list goes on, and without a systematic analysis, we are forced to speculate about the degree to which serendipity has driven innovation over time. In each of these cases, however, it is worth noting that the inventor also had a mind prepared to recognize the discovery embedded in chance observation. Goodyear capitalized on luck, but his prior exposure at the Roxbury India Rubber Company had made him aware of their rubber problems. With

the right cultural exposure, one person's mistake is another's serendipitous discovery.

So how can innovations occur without a conscious inventor? Complex artefacts can evolve without a 'designer' through three key processes:

- incremental improvement
- recombination of existing elements
- selection of new or modified artefacts

Every mythologized invention can be explained through the framework presented in Figure 4.10. Edison did not invent the light bulb. It was only an incremental innovation brought about by recombining existing ideas, which then survived selection and was finally accepted by the consumer. Fleming's 'invention' of penicillin was a fortuitous accident. James Watt was not the inventor of the steam engine – he made an incremental, albeit important, improvement on the existing steam engine architecture. Steve Jobs did not invent anything, although, just like Edison, his penchant for patenting every tiny improvement arguably created barriers for other innovations to take place.

It does not follow from the above that any kind of strategy or planning is useless as far innovation is concerned. It has been shown, again in the anthropological literature, that complex and large societies produce complex technologies. The structure and the size of the community, the group or tribe affect the intensity of innovation within them. As far as innovation is concerned, context is king, and that is where the focus should firmly be.

We need to stop paying obeisance to the Cult of the Individual in innovation studies. We also need to move away from abstract economics to explain how innovation takes place in the real world. Evolutionary anthropology, which is concerned with real human behaviour, has much to offer in this regard.

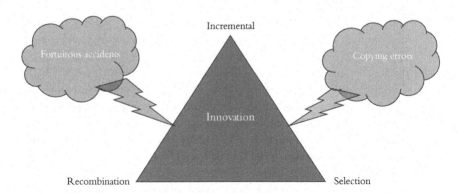

FIGURE 4.10 The evolutionary anthropological perspective on innovation

CASE STUDY 4.1: THE RISE OF NETFLIX AND THE FALL OF BLOCKBUSTER

When The Buggles brought out their epic pop song 'Video Killed the Radio Star' in 1979, the band could not yet foresee how video itself would eventually come to an end. The song's lyrics show a great deal of nostalgia for a bygone era. And it shows how the change in preferences and taste is also an inspiration to song-writers to cope with the speed of ongoing changes.

A change in businesses is not new. The story of Netflix and Blockbuster bears some lessons that inspire commentators to frequently refer to the biblical parable of David and Goliath. Another aspect of the David and Goliath story shares similarity with Netflix. David shoots Goliath with his sling, killing Goliath instantly. Some narratives appear to change quickly.

Netflix[1] – founded in 1997, in Scotts Valley, California – is a prime example of a startup initiated by a grave disappointment over services provided by the incumbent company, Blockbuster.

Within five years after foundation, Netflix obtained a listing on the NASDAQ stock exchange. For the year 2019, it achieved a profit of US$1.9 billion on a turnover of US$20.2 billion.

The company was founded by Marc Randolph and Reed Hastings, after Hastings was fined for the late return of a rental movie. Out of this disappointment, the founders developed a deep desire to change the status quo.

In the beginning, the company offered to home deliver rental DVDs for an undetermined time. Its iconic red envelops quickly became a design feature for home delivery.

However, changes in postal delivery services affected the firm.[2] As such, the move into video-streaming services in 2007 was started in addition to the established core business of DVD-rental services. Within a few years after starting its video-on-demand services, the company announced in September 2011 – within barely four years of operating its streaming services – that it was separating its postal-rental services from its streaming activities. The DVD-rental part was renamed Qwikster and was to continue its operation in parallel. The video-on-demand activities remained within the realm of Netflix. However, this separation of services did not last long. In fact, only weeks after the separation was announced, the Qwikster initiative was cancelled even before being launched.

The fight for the market of watching movies from your sofa

The success of Netflix and the company's growing customer subscription base reflected a shift in consumer preferences that went deeper than merely catering for increased demands for convenience.

During the late 1990s and in early 2000, one company dominated the market of watching videos at home. Through its chain of franchise-stores, the company Blockbuster ran more than 4,500 rental shops at its peak in 2004 in the US alone. Worldwide, more than 9,000 shops displayed the blue and yellow logo of Blockbuster LLC.[3]

Through an extended network of rental shops Blockbuster offered VHS-videos to its customers. The industry standard of watching movies at home in the late 1990s was the VHS-video tape which was firmly in the hands of Blockbuster. Not many customers owned a DVD-player back in those days. Although the market size of rental DVDs was limited, Netflix dared to take a bet on the future. Netflix partnered up with companies that produce DVD players and offered a free trial when purchasing a new DVD player. The bet on the future played out rather well for Netflix. In the first instance, Netflix offered its services for a fixed amount per month with unlimited DVD rental – and most important to the founders: no late-delivery fee!

Netflix's bet on the future industry standard played out rather quickly. During the early 2000s the use of DVDs spread across the market. More and more customers were willing to shift towards the new devices and Netflix became an option to consider.

In the meantime, Netflix approached Blockbuster to offer itself for sale to the media-monopolist; yet Blockbuster refused. This offer is widely used as an example of two opposing views on the future. Where Netflix saw its future on the yet emerging niche market of online-platform services, the incumbent behemoth Blockbuster aimed to protect its fortress of brick-and-mortar stores against competition.[4]

Within six years of foundation, Netflix became profitable in 2003. And the company achieved its hallmark of 1 million subscribers. One year later, Blockbuster started its own postal-rent-service to conquer its smaller competitor and tap into the new industry standard of DVDs.

However, the game was still one of David against Goliath and the chances of Netflix succeeding were rather limited. Yet, Netflix was able to increase its market share. Customers changed VHS for DVD players and grew accustomed to mail-order services and ordering products via the internet. To Netflix, the global trend to online business platforms was nothing new. For Blockbuster, however, the change in customer preferences and technology standards played havoc. In 2007, Netflix announced its online streaming services. In 2010, Netflix dominated the market for home-entertainment movies with increasing profits.

Video may have killed the radio star, but this does not say much for its own chance of survival. In 2010, Blockbuster filed for bankruptcy.

The market of watching movies at home by renting videos or DVDs through a chain of stores became as outdated as thinking about listing to radio broadcasts for home entertainment – as The Buggles' song 'video killed the radio star' suggested some decades ago. The story of Netflix seems to illustrate some aspects worth emphasizing. No one knows the future. And those who pretend to know simply ignore this very fact. In the end, it seems that a few skills in business work out pretty well.

First, Netflix showed responsiveness to changing market demands. In other words, it showed **adaptability**. One movie that illustrates this concept, starring Meryl Streep and Nicolas Cage is the comedy-drama meta-movie 'Adaptation' of 2002.

The movie seems to foreshadow the upcoming changes in rental-services ongoing in the early 2000s. Nicolas Cage plays a screenwriter who suffers from writer's block after realizing that the book *The Orchid Thief* that he intends to write a movie script about simply has no clear narrative nor is it practically possible to base a movie on this novel. Little in his life seems to make sense. Eventually, he includes himself as character in his own script ... [eds: Stop here – Spoiler alert!]

A second element, besides the ability to adapt to changing circumstances and to anticipate unfolding changes in consumer preferences, is illustrated by the company's ability to dive into yet uncharted waters.

The company did not stop with rental-services or streaming-on-demand movies. Eventually, Netflix produced its own content. In 2013, Kevin Spacey was starring in the first Netflix production, 'House of Cards'. Until the withdrawal of the actor due to accusations of sexual harassment in 2017, the TV series received numerous awards. One year later, in November 2018, the last season was released. By then, the company had established itself with a strong reputation of own content production.

On the invention of binge watching, or, the story of the Netflix recommendation system

Due to the early success of 'House of Cards', Netflix extensively invested in its own content. Content that proved remarkably successful with a range of award-winning movies, documentaries and TV shows. However, providing too much content might leave some customers feeling drowned in way too many options. One of the pivotal elements to keeping customers engaged with its service-offering happens through its recommendation system.

> Our business is a subscription service model that offers personalized recommendations, to help you find shows and movies of interest to you. To do this we have created a proprietary, complex recommendations system.
> (Netflix company website[5])

Netflix offers a glimpse behind the curtain of its algorithm. To estimate the likelihood of a potential suggestion for its customers, the company analyses viewing history, age and gender, rating preferences and similarities with other subscribers of its services. Besides these obvious elements, other inputs to the company's recommendation system are derived from the time of watching, the type of device used and how long someone watches. As such, the company is able to provide detailed suggestions to keep customers attracted. Every single visit to the company's website improves the level of recommendations as the company website continues to illustrate:

> Our data, algorithms, and computation systems continue to feed into each other to produce fresh recommendations to provide you with a product that brings you joy.

For now, it appears that Netflix did a tremendous job in bringing joy to its customers. The company's market capitalization amounted to US$146.5 billion in January 2020.

The way forward

The remarkable success of Netflix, attracted more than just a few spectators. As CNN, an American television channel owned by AT&T's WarnerMedia, another media company, titled one of their editorials in 2017, ' "House of Cards" made Netflix a powerhouse. What now?'[6] It appears that the biggest threat to the company's success was considered a breach with media production outlets such as Disney's repository of Pixar, Lucasfilm and Marvel films.

As such, Netflix seems to answer the question, 'What now?' by heavily investing in exclusive content on the firm's platform. It remains open to question whether the apparent fate of the company to outsmart its competitors is indeed eternal. How video killed the radio star bears an obvious nostalgia for its listeners. To many movie-lovers around the globe, the story of the empire carrying the seed of its own demise in its rising, however, may seem far too common to neglect. It remains to be seen how the company will adapt to the future.

Pointers to strategic conversation

1. How did Netflix disrupt Blockbuster's business model?
2. Was the Netflix business model based on new technologies or existing ones?
3. What kind of innovation does Netflix specialize in?
4. We know innovation is recombination of resources and capabilities. Which resources and capabilities did Netflix recombine and how?

Sources

[1] Netflix company website – www.netflix.com
[2] NBC News.com – Netflix is the big loser in Postal Service changes, 30 March 2020: www.nbcnews.com/id/36100708/ns/business-the_big_money/t/netflix-big-loser-postal-service-changes/#.XoWn0i9Y50s

[3] Blockbuster company website – www.blockbuster.com

[4] Forbes – A Look Back at Why Blockbuster Really Failed and Why It Didn't Have To – 5 September 2014: www.forbes.com/sites/gregsatell/2014/09/05/a-look-back-at-why-blockbuster-really-failed-and-why-it-didnt-have-to/#4d364ec71d64

[5] Netflix company website – How Netflix's Recommendations System Works: https://help.netflix.com/en/node/100639

[6] CNN Business, 'House of Cards' made Netflix a powerhouse. What now? 1 November 2017: https://money.cnn.com/2017/11/01/investing/netflix-stock-house-of-cards-kevin-spacey/index.html

CASE STUDY 4.2: SAMSUNG

About one out of five new smartphones bought in 2019[1] displayed the logo of the South Korean business conglomerate, Samsung Electronics Co. Ltd. In 2019, the company achieved a total revenue of about 230 trillion won, about US$198 billion.

Founded in 1969, the company went on to outgrow most of its competitors in the highly competitive market of communication equipment and electronics.[2] This is done through three business divisions,[3] each grouped around a set of product-specific characteristics. Consumer electronics, for example, comprising home appliances ranging from television sets and printers to washing machines and refrigerators. A second division produces memory and large-scale integrated circuits to business clients. Most prolific to the general public is the company's third division, Information Technology & Mobile Communications, producing smartphones and communication systems. As such, the company holds a diverse product portfolio, catering to the specific demands of both retail and business clients.

Strategy and innovation

It is no surprise that the letter to shareholders for the year 2019 expresses the company's view on its future in clear words.

> Our world is transitioning into an era of intelligence and innovation based on data and led by 5G and AI technology. Seismic changes seem imminent considering ongoing innovations in disruptive technologies and ever-increasing corporate competition.
>
> (Samsung Investor Relations, Letter to the Shareholders 2019)[4]

How the company is going to respond to those seismic changes becomes clear when the letter continues: 'Planning to maintain our leadership role regardless of the changes in the environment, we are aggressively investing in R&R'. The company's aggressive investing combines internal R&D activities of its in-house department with an extended network of strategic collaboration through four channels. Around the four elements of partnerships, ventures, accelerators and acquisitions,[5] Samsung creates a framework that provides both the scale and scope to identify promising new ventures at an early stage and provide the option to develop promising new initiatives into new products or service-offerings.

One example of the company's approach to innovation relates to its research on semiconductors:

> To put the principles of Open Innovation into operation, Samsung adopts a multi-pronged approach that involves participation in global consortiums, forging links between the industry and top universities, cooperation with vendors, and running leading-edge overseas research centers.
>
> (Samsung Semiconductor, company website)[6]

Samsung's role in global consortiums is aimed to foster 'synthesizing divergent viewpoints from other participants' with the intention to develop its efforts into a mutually beneficial business ecosystem to its partners, as the statement continues. The importance of strategic alliances between industry and academia is emphasized to ensure an early view on emerging future trends in technology. Ensuring timely access to new developments in the markets is particularly important in industry sectors with fast and substantial changes in products, processes and competition. The traditional position of vendors is also enhanced by close cooperation to ensure high quality standards of materials, components and supplier processes. Finally, overseas research centres are used by Samsung to increase its R&D operations, emphasizing areas of specific technologies and developing those research projects and findings into tangible products and service offerings.

'Startups: The Secret Ingredient of Samsung's Open Innovation'[7]

The Samsung Global Innovation Center (GIC), founded in 2013, had a clearly Herculean task. The Center's mission is nothing less than to guide Samsung's transformation from a hardware production company into one 'that also leads in software and services', as a press release in 2015 announced. To publicly formulate a strategic mission of this magnitude reflects the company's confidence in its own capabilities. Hence, Samsung does not consider its legacy of a South Korean business conglomerate, a so-called *chaebol*, as a disadvantage to evolve into new directions. As the press release continues, the role of GIC is outlined as 'cultivating deep relationships with startup ecosystems in Silicon Valley, New York City and around the globe'. A company that is historically equipped to initiate, maintain and organize processes within one business group is mostly likely also able to extend those capabilities towards collaborative alliances. As such, organizational patterns of business group formation show similarities with patterns of strategic innovation through alliance networks. However, to ensure a sustainable organizational repository of strategic collaboration, the company's efforts to orchestrate multiple channels of innovation strongly relies on a prolific foundation of organizational, cultural and historic conditionalities.

The art of collaborating

Samsung is well experienced to orchestrate its innovation efforts across a range of partners and initiatives.[8] Interestingly enough, Samsung shares those experiences and the lessons the company learned through its online Newsroom. One of the company's articles reveals how Samsung views its own activities in the light of its strategic innovation policy. In 'How Samsung is Collaborating for the Future of Work', the company describes its motivation and how it engages with partners to advance its strategic position.

However, all partnerships share a pivotal element. To effectively engage with each other, a partnership has to provide mutual benefits to each partner individually. In a market place where competition is fierce, to solve this paradox requires some careful attention. Strategic partnerships with Microsoft and Cisco display the ubiquity of this approach within the same sector. Joining forces to mutually advance one's own strategic aims does not contradict with an individual company's long-term interests. As such, considerable efforts are dedicated to orchestrate strategic collaboration.

> Samsung and Microsoft share a commitment to open collaboration and are continually looking for new ways to deliver the best productivity experiences across devices, applications and services.
> (Rob Howard, Senior Director, Microsoft)
> (in, Samsung Newsroom, 2019)

Every act of collaboration – either through strategic partnerships, active collaboration by means of accelerator programmes or venture capital investments – requires managerial efforts to formulate and execute a strategy that ensures mutual benefits among its partners. Only then are the different forms of collaboration able to achieve a sustainable and long-lasting strategic advantage to its partners. One example of this awareness to emphasize long-term interests, relates to the Samsung Knox Partner Program.[9] Samsung provides adequate partners with access to its development environment for enterprise services. This programme not only provides Samsung with early access to new and potentially lucrative business areas, but it also provides its potential programme partners with access to a resourceful and experienced product development organization.

The view from the sideline

The Open Innovation approach to strategic development received attention from corporations, consulting firms and academics alike. In 2017, Accenture, a technology consulting firm, had a look at one of Samsung's crowd-sourcing contests for the ARTIK-platform.[10] Through this initiative, the company invited 500 external app developers to submit app prototypes to the ARTIK-project, an Internet-of-Things (IoT) innovation area.

Historically, Samsung's strategic strength was the development of technology hardware appliances and infrastructure. However, 'finding novel and useful complementary IoT applications for markets such as consumer wearable or high-end industry uses lay outside Samsung's core competencies' as Accenture outlines. The report continues in addressing the specific conditions under which Samsung chose to out-source the development of app-prototypes to the global software ecosystem of external developers. One important reason that the consulting firm identified was the characteristic of the ARTIK platform itself. The ARTIK problem 'had a manageable degree of complexity but a high degree of knowledge hiddenness' as Accenture revealed. The platform's version was then still in a developmental and pre-production, beta stage. The company lacked pivotal knowledge of the future direction the hosting platform and applications would have to align with.

In addition to the necessity to reach out to external developers, a second element was for Samsung to opt for a developmental approach based on the company's practical experience in modular software development kits and the ability to closely manage relationships with external parties.

From initiating collaboration to sustain collaborators' commitments at the ARTIK-platform

Reaching out to a global community of experienced app developers was only the first step of Samsung's innovation strategy for the ARTIK-platform. After the initiation, the company found early evidence supporting the view to extend the collaboration beyond the early phase of exploring directions and development areas. To sustain the commitment of the app-developers involved in the contest became a task that included 'to manage knowledge sharing before the platform's concept had been proved', as Accenture identified.

Working on a beta-version of an IoT-platform – that was yet itself subject to changes in its coding and structure – required the company to clearly outline the software's key requirements together with the practical rationales for the app developers to align with during the contest.

In 2015, the company announced publicly how it saw its innovation strategy. In particular, the role of startups is emphasized by the company. Access to the products and services offered by startups becomes possible through partnership programmes for co-developing software, as strategic investment or through the company's role in accelerator programmes across the globe.

Pointers to strategic conversation

1. What are the difficulties, from the firm perspective, in pursuing an open innovation approach?
2. What benefits have accrued to Samsung from its open innovation approach?
3. What are the benefits of a closed approach in innovation?
4. Going forward, should Samsung pursue a more open or closed approach to innovation?

Sources

[1] Statista – Smartphone market share worldwide by vendor 2009–2019: www. statista.com/statistics/271496/global-market-share-held-by-smartphone-vendors-since-4th-quarter-2009/

[2] Bloomberg – Samsung company profile: www.bloomberg.com/profile/company/005930:KS

[3] MarketsInsider – Samsung company profile: https://markets.businessinsider.com/stocks/samsung/company-profile

[4] Samsung Investor Relations – company website: www.samsung.com/global/ir/governance-csr/ceo-msg/

[5] Viima.comCollaboration–www.viima.com/blog/16-examples-of-open-innovation-what-can-we-learn-from-them

[6] Samsung Semiconductor – company website: www.samsung.com/semiconductor/about-us/open-innovation/

[7] Samsung Newsroom – Press release 21 September 2015: https://news.samsung.com/global/startups-the-secret-ingredient-of-samsungs-open-innovation

[8] Samsung Newsroom – Press release 31 October 2019: https://news.samsung.com/global/how-samsung-is-collaborating-for-the-future-of-work

[9] Samsung Knox Partner Program – company website: https://partner.samsungknox.com

[10] Accenture report 'Open Innovation at Samsung, 2017': www.accenture.com/t00010101t000000__w__/gb-en/_acnmedia/pdf-43/accenture-open-innovation-at-samsung.pdf

Conclusion

Recombination is the main process through which innovation materializes. This chapter has shown that innovation happens at various levels and it can be looked at from different perspectives. Moreover, these perspectives are interlinked in many ways. Innovation at a micro level, for example, is affected by the dynamics that are ongoing at a more macro level. This chapter has provided a rounded perspective on innovation that encompasses national, firm and individual levels.

Notes

1 The 'father' of innovation studies, Joseph Schumpeter underlined this point in his classic book *The Theory of Economic Development*, published in 1934. 'Innovation is resource recombination', Schumpeter said.
2 See Muthukrishna and Henrich, 2016. They argue that our evolved brains are adapted for social learning, and when that is applied within a social context, innovation is inevitable.
3 See North, 1991 for a detailed exposition of the idea of institutions as 'rules of the game'.
4 The idea gathered steam after the end of the Second World War and with the publication of Vannevar Bush's report *Science: The Endless Frontier* (1945).
5 For a detailed overview of the idea of National Innovation System, see Freeman, 1995.
6 The systemic perspective on innovation can be traced back to the nineteenth century writings of Friedrich List, the German economist. Chris Freeman in the early 1980s took on some of List's insights and popularized the idea of the national innovation system. See Freeman, 1995.
7 See Guston and Keniston (1994).
8 See Gibbons et al. (1994).
9 See Etzkowitz and Leydesdroff (2000).
10 Data on UK university spinouts can be found at this link: www.hesa.ac.uk/data-and-analysis/business-community/ip-and-startups.
11 It is important to keep in mind that the role of universities is multifaceted within the national innovation system with university spinouts being just one of them. See Datta et al. (2019) for a classification of the different contributions that universities make within the innovation system.
12 See Hall (2001).
13 See Christensen (1992).
14 See Klepper (1996).
15 For example, the bread or rice industries do not follow the Industry Life Cycle patterns; these are not technology intensive and they serve basic needs.
16 See Suarez and Utterback (1993).
17 See Christensen (1997).
18 The turnaround time of an aircraft is defined as the time that passes from when an aircraft lands until it takes off again for a new flight.
19 See Rosenberg (1994).
20 The empirical evidence on the positive correlation between IPR and innovation is not clear cut. On many occasions it has been found that IPRs reduce, rather than accelerate, innovation. See for example Williams, 2013.

21 For a good overview of the two alternate models of innovation, see Von Hippel and Krogh, 2003.
22 See Von Hippel (1986).
23 Arthur Koestler (1964) showed how the underlying processes that underpin creativity in humour, science and the arts are essentially the same.
24 See Muthukrishna and Henrich (2016).

Further reading

Bush, V. (1945). *Science: The endless frontier.* Washington, DC: United States Government Printing Office.

Chesbrough, H. W., & Appleyard, M. M. (2007). Open innovation and strategy. *California management review, 50*(1), 57–76.

Christensen, C. M. (1992). Exploring the limits of the technology S-curve. Part I: component technologies. *Production and operations management, 1*(4), 334–357.

Christensen, C. M. (1997). *The innovator's dilemma: When new technologies cause great firms to fail.* Boston, MA: Harvard Business School Press.

Datta, S., Saad, M., & Sarpong, D. (2019). National systems of innovation, innovation niches, and diversity in university systems. *Technological forecasting and social change,* 143(C), 27–36.

Etzkowitz, H., & Leydesdorff, L. (2000). The dynamics of innovation: from National Systems and 'Mode 2' to a Triple Helix of university–industry–government relations. *Research policy, 29*(2), 109–123.

Freeman, C. (1995). The 'National System of Innovation' in historical perspective. *Cambridge journal of economics, 19*(1), 5–24.

Galvao, A., Mascarenhas, C., Marques, C., Ferreira, J., & Ratten, V. (2019). Triple helix and its evolution: a systematic literature review. *Journal of science and technology policy management, 10*(3), 812–833.

Gibbons, M. (Ed.). (1994). *The new production of knowledge: The dynamics of science and research in contemporary societies.* London: Sage.

Guston, D. H., & Keniston, K. (Eds.) (1994). *The fragile contract: University science and the federal government.* Cambridge, MA: MIT Press.

Hall, P. (2001). *Cities in civilisation.* New York: Fromm International.

Klepper, S. (1996). Entry, exit, growth, and innovation over the product life cycle. *The American economic review, 86*(3), 562–583.

Koestler, A. (1964). *The act of creation.* London: Hutchinson.

Leydesdorff, L. (2010). The knowledge-based economy and the triple helix model. *Annual review of information science and technology 44*, 367–417.

Muthukrishna, M., & Henrich, J. (2016). Innovation in the collective brain. *Philosophical transactions of the Royal Society B: Biological sciences, 371*(1690), 20150192.

North, D. C. (1991). Institutions. *Journal of economic perspectives, 5*(1), 97–112.

Rosenberg, N. (1994). *Exploring the black box: Technology, economics, and history.* Cambridge: Cambridge University Press.

Schumpeter, J. (1934). *The theory of economic development.* Cambridge, MA: Harvard University Press.

Stark, J. (2015). Product lifecycle management. In *Product lifecycle management (Volume 1)* (pp. 1–29). Cham: Springer.

Suarez, F., & Utterback, J. (1993). Patterns of industrial evolution, dominant designs, and firms' survival. *Research on technological innovation, management and policy, 5*, 47–87.

Von Hippel, E. (1986). Lead users: a source of novel product concepts. *Management science*, *32*(7), 791–805.

Von Hippel, E., & Krogh, G. V. (2003). Open source software and the 'private-collective' innovation model: Issues for organization science. *Organization science*, *14*(2), 209–223.

Williams, H. L. (2013). Intellectual property rights and innovation: Evidence from the human genome. *Journal of political economy*, *121*(1), 1–27.

5

REACH

Going global

The majority of firms are born local and stay local. Some are born local and then become global. Only a select few are born global. This chapter is about the reach of the firm, the geographical extent of its operations. Reach is about internationalization. It is about why firms become transnational companies and how that extra reach helps them in achieving competitive success.

Why all firms are not multinationals

We start with a counterintuitive question. Why aren't all firms global? One normally assumes that it makes economic sense to start local and then gradually increase reach, but let's pause and think about this for a moment. Firms are capitalist entities. Their main purpose is to maximize profit for the shareholders. How can you increase profits? There are essentially three ways: a) increase sales while keeping production costs steady, or b) decrease cost of production while keeping sales steady, or c) do both – increase sales and decrease costs.

Increasing the reach of the firm beyond national borders helps to achieve both – firms can access new markets and increase sales, and they can access more and better quality of factors of production, comprising for example labour, capital, land and technology. And reduce costs more efficiently. So, if profit maximization is the ultimate goal, all firms should be transnational. Yet, we find plenty of local firms. Why?

Your intuitive answer to this question will be straightforward: It is difficult. It is not an easy job to operate on a transnational basis. Your intuition in this case is right. International business scholars have defined this as **Liability of Foreignness.**[1] These are the additional costs that firms incur when they operate outside their home nation. A local firm in India, for example, knows the local conditions far better than a foreign company with no previous exposure to the country. This local knowledge may relate to indigenous business practices, native language, government policies and others. These are the natural advantages that local players enjoy over their foreign rivals. So, for a foreign firm to successfully compete in an overseas market, it must possess some firm-specific resources and capabilities that allow it to overcome these natural barriers to entry.

We can surmise from the above that although most firms would like to be global, not all of them possess the organizational advantages that would allow the offset of Liability of Foreignness and, as a consequence, many are forced to remain as domestic players.

Drivers of reach: Motivations for going global

Why do firms want to become transnational? We have already said that the main reason is to increase profits. Now let's break that down to its constitutive elements. There are two main motivations:[2]

a. Resource acquisition
b. Market penetration

Resource acquisition

Here, the firm is oriented towards acquisitions of productive resources. This may include land, labour, capital and technology. A domestic firm has access to local factors of production. A multinational firm can tap into those beyond national borders. We may reflect on the resource-based view (RBV) of the firm here (Chapter 3: Resources). If firm-specific resources are the basis of competitive success, then it is critical that companies acquire the right kind of resources, and their chances of doing this increase manifold when they look beyond their own national boundaries.

It is impossible to provide an exhaustive list of resources that motivates firms to go international, but the main ones are the following:

a. Labour: both skilled and unskilled
b. Knowledge: both tacit and codified
c. Land
d. Capital

Firms are often forced to go overseas when they face constraints at home in terms of accessing the factors of production that are essential for growth (see Table 5.1). In terms of UNCTAD's **Transnationality Index**, the most 'transnational' firms are not from the largest economies, rather they are typically from small nation-states.

Toyota would have never become the huge company it is now had it remained based only in Japan. The same goes for Nokia in Finland and IKEA in Sweden. Companies that want to achieve global competitiveness but are based in small economies have more reasons to extend their reach, to transnationalize their operations.

TABLE 5.1 UNCTAD's Transnationality Index of non-financial transnational corporations, 2012

TNI*	Corporation	Home economy	Industry
1	Nestlé SA	Switzerland	Food, beverages and tobacco
2	Anglo American plc	United Kingdom	Mining & quarrying
3	Xstrata PLC	Switzerland	Mining & quarrying
4	Anheuser-Busch InBev NV	Belgium	Food, beverages and tobacco
5	ABB Ltd	Switzerland	Engineering services
6	ArcelorMittal	Luxembourg	Metal and metal products
7	Linde AG	Germany	Chemicals
8	Vodafone Group Plc	United Kingdom	Telecommunications
9	Schneider Electric SA	France	Electricity, gas and water
10	WPP PLC	United Kingdom	Business services

Source: UNCTAD, official website, ranked by TNI: https://unctad.org/Sections/dite_dir/docs/WIR2013/WIR13_webtab28.xls

The TNI, the Transnationality Index, is calculated as the average of the following three ratios: foreign assets to total assets, foreign sales to total sales and foreign employment to total employment.

Market penetration

Assuming your profit margins are stable, the main way to increase overall profitability of the firm is to increase sales. Firms that can sell globally would obviously be in a better position than those who are able to only sell nationally or locally.

The motivation to tap into new markets overseas is influenced by the size of the targeted markets. Which country did Toyota target for exports? In 1957 Toyota started exporting cars to the United States, the first overseas country it targeted. The reason was obvious; the United States represented the most attractive market for Toyota.

The factors that determine market potential are:

a. GDP per capita
b. Demography
c. Institutions, the 'rules of the game'
d. Transparency level

Extending reach: The internationalization process

The incremental approach

How do firms internationalize their operations? The most popular way of extending reach is the **Incremental Approach**, also called the **Stage Model of Internationalization**.[3] The incremental approach in internationalization is predicated on a simple idea – take one step at a time into the unknown. Internationalization means venturing into unfamiliar territories. The uncertainty can be unpacked into two distinct classes, namely the **modes of internationationalization** and **markets.**

Modes of internationalization

Firms can internationalize their operations through various modes. The obvious first step is to produce in the home nation and **export** a part of the production to other countries. Another way to internationalize operations is to appoint **overseas agents** who secure business on your behalf. Firms can also **license** their intellectual properties to international firms and earn royalties from such licensing arrangements. On the production side, firms can **outsource** their production to foreign partners. And, they can set up their **own production** units overseas.

The uncertainty level goes up through the modes as shown in Figure 5.1.

Markets

Foreign markets are unknown entities. They portend all sorts of uncertainties. But are all foreign markets equally uncertain? In international business, the geographic distance between two countries can be different from the **'psychic distance'** that separates them. Psychic distance is how much psychologically close or distant the citizens of one country feel to another nation (see Figure 5.2). The UK and Australia are separated by great geographical distance; 9,443 miles to be exact. Yet due to shared history, institutions and cultural practices these two nations are psychically quite close to each other. One can cogently argue that the UK is psychically closer to Australia than it is to some European nations, although geographically, the UK is part of the European continent.

A complex array of factors makes up the psychic distance. The CAGE framework specifies most of these factors.[4]

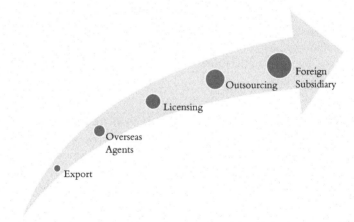

FIGURE 5.1 Export – overseas agents – licensing – outsourcing – foreign subsidiaries

FIGURE 5.2 CAGE framework

When looking to venture into foreign markets, firms unsurprisingly first look at 'psychically close' countries. Important to note here, is that often geographical and psychic distances overlap each other. Not really surprising, as you tend to know your neighbours better than people residing at the other end of the town. The psychic distance between the Nordic countries is small, and so is the geographical distance. Yet, as we have seen in the case of the UK and Australia, the geographic and the psychic distances between two can be radically divergent.

Historically, two patterns have been observed in the internationalization process of firms. First, they enter markets sequentially, that is, they will enter Country A, and only after spending a solid time developing their operations in that country, will they venture into Country B. Second, they choose psychically close countries at the initial stages and only when they become comfortable in international operations, will they proceed towards the psychically more distant ones.

So, we have seen that firms adopt the incremental approach on two dimensions – the modes of internationalization and the entry into new markets (see Figure 5.3).

'Born global' firms

While the incremental approach is the norm when it comes to internationalization, there are always exceptions. Not all firms' internationalization efforts follow the stage model. Some firms go directly to setting up of sales offices overseas rather than

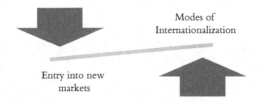

Modes of
Internationalization

Entry into new
markets

FIGURE 5.3 The incremental approach

testing the waters first with exports. Others go straight to international production. A few go to international production right at the inception; that is, they start serving and producing in foreign locations even before they have started operations in the home nation. These firms are called 'born-globals'.[5]

So, how do born-globals circumvent the logic of incrementalism? To answer that question, we have to appreciate the fact that the incremental approach is a solution to an organizational knowledge problem. Faced with the lack of knowledge about conditions prevalent in foreign locations, firm move cautiously in their internationalization efforts. But, if firms have organizational resources that make them confident about international operations, they can adopt a 'big bang' approach; hence, they can be born-globals.[6]

To be more specific, consider a new firm based in the UK with three partners, one of them a native, the other two expatriates settled in the country – one from Germany the other from China. While their main market for the new product is in the UK, they need to design their new product, and the best designers are based in Germany. They also then would need to produce their products in volume, and for that the most cost-efficient location is China. The incremental approach would involve designing the product and producing it initially in the home nation and then gradually extend the reach of the firm. But in this specific case, the firm has organizational knowledge of the local conditions in Germany and China, due to the two expatriate partners, and feels confident enough to be a born-global firm. They successfully get the new product designed in Germany, produce it in volume in China and sell their products in Europe. This is a real example. The German expatriate entrepreneur is an ex-student of one of the authors.

India, in recent years, has produced lots of born-global IT firms. Even before there was an IT software home market in India, software firms from the country were servicing customers in North America and Europe. How was that possible? Many of the first-generation Indian IT-entrepreneurs either received their higher education from, or have worked as a professional in North America or Europe. When India started liberalizing its economy from early 1990 onward, these would-be IT-entrepreneurs consecutively returned to their home nation to set up businesses in places like Pune, Hyderabad, Gurgaon and Bangalore. They leveraged their contacts in North America and Europe to secure business from these lucrative markets. Again here, organizational knowledge helped these IT firms in India to become born-globals.

Complexities of extensive reach

We have established that multinationals have an economic advantage over domestic firms. But this advantage comes at a price, which is the added complexity that they have to deal with. Organizing economic activities on a transnational basis is undoubtedly more complicated than running a local grocery shop. The added complexities of transnational operations arise out of the **pressure of global integration** and the need for **local responsiveness**.[7]

Pressure for global integration

In some industries, the need for global integration is paramount. The steel industry is a prime example of this. If you are running a large integrated steel manufacturing unit, you need to produce in a location that not only has access to the necessary raw materials but also low costs of labour and good infrastructure. The textile industry is another good example. The manufacturing of textile garments has shifted almost entirely to some nations because of the requirement and availability of low cost semi-skilled labour. If you want to be a major competitor in the garment industry you simply cannot afford to remain local or national, you must extend your reach beyond your nation's borders.

Need for local responsiveness

Thinking of selling your standard European hamburgers in India? Think again. The McDonald's menu in India is significantly different from that in the UK. There isn't a single beef product on the Indian McDonald's menu. The company had to respond to local tastes and preferences. Life would have been much simpler for McDonald's if it could offer one standardized menu across the globe, but the downside of extending your reach is that local conditions necessitate customization of your products, and that acts as a constraint on internationalization. Some industries need more customization than others. A smartphone in terms of its hardware is a highly standardized product. Smartphones are produced in cost efficient locations and exported around the world. But fiscal policies vary significantly across nation-states. So, there are multinational tax consultancies, but they generally hire local specialists to deliver services to local clients.

Based on these two drivers, firms adopt different approaches to internationalization. There are four basic approaches:

a. Export based
b. Production based
c. Customization based
d. Production and customization based

Export-based internationalization

This involves producing in the home nation and exporting to the rest of the world. In terms of complexity, this ranks lowest among the different approaches to internationalization. But it is also most difficult to pull-off successfully. Think of a firm that can avoid full-fledged internationalization – setting up sales offices and shifting production overseas – and yet can successfully compete with other more transnationalized firms in the market. Facebook in its initial years was based wholly in the Boston area in the United States while its services were being consumed all over the world. So, one can suggest that in the initial years Facebook pursued an export-based internationalization, but over the years that approach changed. Facebook today is very much a multinational company.

Production-based internationalization

Firms adopt production-based internationalization typically, but not always, when the cost pressures are high. Steel and textiles industries operate under great cost pressure, and we have seen firms operating in these industries migrating to cost-efficient locations across the globe. But sometimes, a production-based approach is pursued to access specialized knowledge that resides outside of the country. Tata Motors, part of the Tata Group from India acquired Jaguar Land Rover, UK, in 2008. Tata's acquisition of Jaguar Land Rover was not based on a cost motive. Rather, Tata wanted to acquire a portfolio of prestigious brands and access the specialized automotive knowledge that resides in the UK[8].

Customization-based internationalization

Customization needs that arise out of local tastes and preferences act as constraints to internationalization efforts of firms. Customizing your product offerings to fit the local conditions of a foreign country requires extensive knowledge of the local conditions. Not all firms are able to pull this off effectively. McDonald's has done this effectively. Multinational accounting and tax consultancy firms like PwC, Deloitte and KPMG must provide services that are tailored to local needs. These firms overcome the barrier to accessing local knowledge by hiring local experts. Investments banking is another industry sector that needs massive customization to cater to local needs.

Production plus customization-based internationalization

The most complex internationalization approach is the one that combines pro-duction and customization. Companies that pursue this approach are truly trans-national. They are operating under both pressures – cost and local responsiveness. Companies in fast moving consumer goods (so-called FMCG companies), like Nestlé and Unilever, pursue this dual approach to internationalization.

Reaching for competitive success

Firms extend their reach for competitive success. That is the primary motivation. But how is this competitive success attained? We saw earlier that local competitors have a natural advantage over foreign firms, which is their knowledge of local conditions. In order to achieve competitive success in a foreign environment, firms need to have **ownership specific advantages** that help them overcome these natural barriers. McDonald's is very successful in China, but they had to overcome competition from Chinese players like 'Kungfu' whose menus reflect the local food preferences more aptly. So why is McDonald's such a big success in China? Its brand, its way of doing business, the standardization of services, all played a part, all part of McDonald's ownership-specific advantages.

But ownership-specific advantages can only deliver success to multinationals if the local conditions allow their effective exploitation. Just imagine, if China did not protect McDonalds's intellectual property rights (IPRs). If any Chinese company could misappropriate the McDonald's brand and call themselves 'McDonalds' or even 'McDonaldz', do you think McDonald's would be a success in China? The answer would be an obvious 'no'. In fact, it would probably not have entered China at all if there was even the slightest chance that its IPRs would not be protected under domestic law.

So, successful foreign production for multinationals requires effective exploitation of ownership-specific advantages which are made possible through favourable local factors.

But we also cannot forget the home national environment of McDonald's. McDonald's core competences were originally developed in the United States. National dynamics (the fast-food culture, vast geographical space which necessitated a franchise-based operation) contributed towards McDonald's international success.

So, we can say that McDonald's success in China is dependent on three distinct elements: its firm-specific advantages, its home country specific advantages, and the host country conditions in China.

The above three factors constitute **a generic model for competitive success at a specific overseas market** (see Figure 5.4).[9] The competitive success at an overseas location is based upon:

a. Firm-specific advantages which allow companies to overcome the natural barriers to internalization that exist in that location.
b. Home country-specific advantages that have strengthened the company's competitive position within that foreign market.
c. Host country conditions that have allowed effective exploitation of the company's firm specific advantages.

But the above does not really explain why multinationals have become the dominant organizational design in international business. From the mid-1980s onwards,

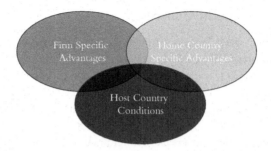

FIGURE 5.4 Determinants of competitive success for a multinational corporation at a foreign location

multinational corporations have become one of the main actors of the global game of business. If you look at the top 100 companies in the world by revenue, they are all multinationals. The trend is well established by now – pure domestic firms are continually squeezed out of business by multinational companies. Clearly, a firm gains an added advantage over domestic firms when it transforms itself into a multinational corporation. But what exactly is this added advantage?

It is the multinational's ability to combine **mobile resources** with **immobile resources** that confers on it the decisive advantage over domestic firms. Mobile resources are those that can be transferred at ease across national boundaries. Mobile resources can include intellectual properties, capital, technology or skilled labour. Immobile resources are factors of production that are specific to a region. These can include unskilled labour or natural resources such as minerals, oil and gas. The domestic firms that are mainly limited to the home nation's factors of production cannot match the ability of multinationals to access factors of production across multiple nations and transfer, combine and recombine those resources across national boundaries.

CASE STUDY 5.1: APPLE, GLOBAL PRODUCTION CHAINS AND COVID-19

On 28 January 2020, Apple Inc. reported a record first quarter results.

The company has a broken book-year and presented the financial results for its fiscal 2020 first quarter ended 28 December 2019 with suitable confidence.[1]

Quarterly revenue amounted to US$91.8 billion, with an increase of 9% from the previous year and an all-time record. Apple's press release takes a view on the company's staggering results:

'Our very strong business performance drove an all-time net income record of $ 22.2 billion and generated operating cash flow of $ 30.5 billion', said Luca Maestri, Apple's CFO. 'We also returned nearly 425 billion to shareholders during the quarter, including $20 billion in share repurchases and $3.5 billion in dividends and equivalents, as we maintain our target of reaching a net cash neutral position over time'.

The press release of the company continues with the words that 'international sales accounted for 61 percent of the quarter's revenue'. The remaining revenue is generated in the company's home market, the United States.

At that time, there wasn't a single cloud on Apple's horizon.

On 2 March 2020 the website Business Insider published an analyst report on Apple addressing the growing concerns of the Covid-19 pandemic for the production of the new iPhone. The analyst Ming-Chi Kuo from KGI Securities estimated that the company would not be able to recover until the second quarter of 2020.[2] In hindsight the analyst's judgement appeared surprisingly optimistic. As a full disclosure to our readers, during the time of writing this business case in April 2020, both the immediate as well as long-term effects of the pandemic and governmental emergency policy have not yet sufficiently materialized to provide a conclusive view on the pandemic's effect on Apple and the general global economy.

However, what become apparent was the fact that Covid-19 became a truly global problem. During the outbreak, companies across the globe were forced to rapidly down-shift their operations, adopt new business processes and remove the dust from their emergency guidelines on how to encounter their worst case scenario.

The pandemic of the coronavirus which causes the illness Covid-19 was quickly considered as the most imminent human and economic disaster since the Second World War. Its long-term effects were expected to be more severe than the effects of 9/11 and the financial crisis after the bankruptcy of Lehman Brothers in September 2008.

One day after the optimistic report by Mr. Kuo, *The Wall Street Journal* followed a more sober reasoning. On 3 March 2020 the newspaper published an online article titled, 'Tim Cook and Apple Bet Everything on China. Then Coronavirus Hit'. The newspaper's editorial leaves little doubt about the company's challenges and continues:[3]

> Quarantines, tariffs and slumping sales have caused agitation about the company's strategy of assembling most of its products there.

By the day, the prospects of a quick recovery and only marginal effects on global production seemed to diminish.

On 20 March 2020, the news-side Business Insider reported that 'Apple's supply chain still struggling to return to normal even as China recovers from the pandemic, report says'.[4]

The news-side refers to an analysts report by Bloomberg,[5] a business information service, that despite the launch of a new iPad Pro and two new

Macs, during the week, Apple Inc. displayed yet an unclear response on the challenges its supply chain faced.

The Bloomberg reports cites Brad Gastwirth, chief technology strategist at Wedbush Securities, that 'While China is improving, the supply chain for the electronics industry may yet see substantial disruptions'. The report continues by emphasizing Apple's 'China-focused supply chain' but did not mention any mitigating practices the company might adopt. Hence, Apple Inc. relies heavily on a global network of component suppliers, assembly and production sites as well as distribution logistics. To a company that is essentially grounded on a global production and distribution structure, one of the firm's core capabilities lies in managing operational processes on a global scale.

Then, on 21 March 2020 *The Economist*, an international weekly newspaper, displayed an illustrative cover-page: 'the world closed'.

The pandemic clearly out-paced much of the global economy; however, the analysis of Mr. Kuo still resonates with analysts' reports on the expected resilience of Apple Inc.

One week later, on 28 March 2020, *The Economist* described in one of its leader articles the global havoc caused by the pandemic so far.

> One reason the state's role has changed so rapidly is that covid-19 spreads like wildfire. In less than four months it has gone from a market in Wuhan to almost every country in the world. The past week logged 253,000 new cases. People are scared of the example of Italy, where almost 74,000 recorded cases have overwhelmed a world-class health system, leading to over 7,500 deaths.

Why do the analyst reports appear to be rather less concerned with the global effect on Apple Inc?

In general, while the severity of Covid-19 came as a surprise, factors influencing global chains of production and distribution are pivotal elements in global companies and are not left to ad hoc measurements and responses.

A policy look on global trade and production

The Organisation for Economic Co-operation and Development (OECD), an intergovernmental economic organization with currently 36 member states, defines global value chains (GVCs) as the business practice in which 'the different stages of the production process are located across different countries'.[6] The OECD further summarizes the commercial reasoning of global value chains as follows:

> Firms try to optimize their production processes by locating the various stages across different sites. The past decades have witnessed a strong trend towards the international dispersion of value chain activities such as design, production, marketing, distribution, etc.

This emergence of GVCs challenges conventional wisdom on how we look at economic globalization and in particular, the policies that we develop around it.

The fact that GVC practices challenge conventional wisdom on economic assumptions and policy guidelines illustrates how strongly GVCs depend on various external factors that are complex to assess. During times of stability and prosperous economic growth, trade policies that foster global production relations are deemed to increase the global economic benefit of the trading countries. During times of instability and external havoc, this 'fragmentation', as the OECD calls it, implies a structural factor that potentially increases the adverse effects of external unrest.

Founded in 1944 at the Bretton Woods Conference, the World Bank is an international financial institution intended to reduce global poverty. The organization provides grants and loans to state governments through a range of global partnerships and initiatives. The World Bank shares a similar view: 'participation in global value chains, the international fragmentation of production, can lead to increased job creation and economic growth'.[7]

The World Bank provides an overview of the relevant factors of GVCs for economic growth, the role of and potential benefits to developing countries and strategies for seizing GVC opportunities. Again, the benefits are clearly outlined yet potential risks that require mitigation are remarkably absent on the topic website.

A third intergovernmental organization that is worthwhile to mention is the World Trade Organization (WTO). On the organization's portal, a broad range of publications and reports is shared on how to measure and analyse global production and trade.[8] The WTO summarizes this pointedly:

> More and more products are 'Made in the World' rather than made in just one economy.

However, it appears that the WTO is more concerned with measuring the effects of global production instead of spending efforts to present a balanced view on risks and benefits of worldwide production processes.

Apple Inc. has a strong legacy of global production processes. Component supply, assembly and production as well as purchase logistics are not limited by national boundaries. As said, Bloomberg emphasized the company's 'China-focused supply chain'. As such, it is worthwhile to have a look at how the company sees its position within the global production context.

Apple's 'Better Together'

Tim Cook, the CEO of Apple, underlines the company's belief about the relationship with its suppliers:[9]

We believe that business, at its best, serves the public good, empowers people around the world, and binds us together as never before.

Around the three elements People, Planet and Progress, the company publishes in its sustainability report the results of ongoing assessments held on production standards at its supplier firms. As the report continues, 'our supply chain is global – so is our responsibility'.

To enable compliance with Apple's operating standards the company issued two documents: the company's Code of Conduct; and the Supplier Responsibility Standard on the Responsible Sourcing of Materials, the Responsible Sourcing Standard. Along three areas of assessment – Labor and Human Rights, Health and Safety and, finally, the Environment – the Code of Conduct is based on general principles of the OECD as well as the United Nations Guiding Principles on Business and Human Rights.

Apple's Supplier Responsibility Progress Report of 2019 illustrates that the company does not neglect any associated risks emerging through a network of fragmented production elements:

> In 2018, we transitioned Apple's Risk Readiness Assessment (RRA) tool to an industry-wide platform. In total, 265 companies that were seeking a tool to assess human rights risks in their sourcing supply chains utilized the tool from a diverse set of industries.

As such, the company outlines that risk management assessments are able to evaluate vital elements in globally dispersed production networks. Through an analysis of standards and principles that include employment conditions, material sourcing and production, the company shows that it has the right tools available to cope with external turmoil and to formulate an adequate response.

It appears that the analysts' reports might not be overly optimistic but reflect a sound understanding of risk assessment standards and production processes.

Whatever the necessary steps will be to cope with the disruption of the Covid-19 pandemic, the answer lies in Apple's view on its production processes: 'Better together'. The way the company responds will be subject to collaborative efforts of the production networks trading partners.

Pointers to strategic conversation

1. What benefits accrue to firms as they extend reach beyond their national boundaries?
2. As companies extend their reach, do they become more vulnerable or more resilient to external shocks?
3. How has Apple's international operations affected its core competences?
4. Can Apple's extensive international reach be its downfall?

Sources

1 Apple company website – Press Release – 'Apple Reports Record First Quarter Results' – 28 January 2020: www.apple.com/newsroom/2020/01/apple-reports-record-first-quarter-results/

2 Business Insider 'The coronavirus outbreak has been hurting Apple's iPhone production, and one of the most accurate analysts says it won't get better until the second quarter of 2020' – 02 March 2020: www.businessinsider.nl/apple-iphone-production-coronavirus-q2-kuo-2020–3?international=true&r=US

3 The *Wall Street Journal*, 'Tim Cook and Apple Bet Everything on China. Then Coronavirus Hit' – 03 March 2020: www.wsj.com/articles/tim-cook-and-apple-bet-everything-on-china-then-coronavirus-hit-11583172087

4 Business Insider 'Apple's supply chain still struggling to return to normal even as China recovers from the pandemic, report says' – 20 March 2020: www.business insider.com/coronavirus-apple-supply-chain-iphone-12-production-2020-3?int ernational=true&r=US&IR=T

5 Bloomberg company website, 'Apple's Supply Chain Woes Linger Even as China Recovers' – 20 March 2020: www.bloomberg.com/news/articles/2020-03-19/apple-s-supply-chain-woes-linger-even-as-china-recovers?sref=9hGJlFio

6 OECD official website – Global Value Chains (GVCs): www.oecd.org/sti/ind/global-value-chains.htm

7 World Bank official website – Global Value Chains: www.worldbank.org/en/topic/global-value-chains

8 World Trade Organization official website – Global Value Chains: www.wto.org/english/res_e/statis_e/miwi_e/miwi_e.htm

9 Apple company website – Supplier Responsibility 2019 Progress Report: www.apple.com/supplier-responsibility/pdf/Apple_SR_2019_Progress_Report.pdf

CASE STUDY 5.2: IKEA

BILLY bookcases, having your kids entertained in Småland and enjoying a plate of kødbollar meatballs after shopping are probably in the top-3 list of associations people have in mind when thinking about the Swedish furniture company, IKEA.

With a net revenue of US$45.4 billion for the year 2019, the business which is held as private company, was founded by Ingvar Kamprad in 1943.[1] Since then, the company extended into much more than a furniture company alone. It became a prime example of adaptability and commercial awareness to changes in living standards around the globe. As such, the company explores complementary ways regarding its current product range that clearly move way beyond the range of self-assembled furniture and home design.

In 2018, a business magazine, Forbes, foreshadowed the company 'transforming into a tech company'.[2] One of the examples relates to IKEA's augmented reality app, through which customers can select products and virtually place them in their own home before actually purchasing a new corner sofa. The appeal to customers is persuasive. What could be more convenient to a prospective customer than virtually putting a new cabinet or kitchen table in your home simply by looking through the augmented reality app on your mobile phone?

The company's move into the area of smart home appliances, for example connected lighting kits and wireless charging furniture, clearly displays that IKEA sees itself as heading towards a future in the technology business. However, technological advancement – such as augmented reality apps or integrated platform solutions to find someone who can help you out in assembling the new BILLY bookcase – requires a careful integration in established operational processes. To integrate technology is not a goal in itself.

IKEA shows how it expects to cope with the accelerating changes imposed on the company through demographic trends, changing living conditions and a global shift towards new standards of servicing retail customers.

IKEA Range & Supply

One organizational unit of IKEA is particularly relevant in managing the different activities within the IKEA Group to ensure sustainable business performances across all production elements. The unit Range & Supply consists of two separate entities: IKEA of Sweden AB, focusing primarily on the range of products offered, and IKEA Supply AG, with its focus on the supply side of production processes. As such, the assignment of Range & Supply is clear:

> IKEA Range & Supply has the responsibility to develop, design, produce and supply home furnishing solutions available to the many people.
>
> (Company website, Inter IKEA Group)[3]

The department's activities are firmly nestled within the strategic framework of IKEA. The holding company Ingka Group controlled 367 of the 422 IKEA stores in 2018. The holding company's Annual Summary & Sustainability Report for the year 2019,[4] summarizes its view on how to sustainably organize the interrelated activities of IKEA across the globe in the following words:

> As a big brand with a big purpose, we have a unique opportunity to really make a positive impact for people and the planet and contribute to wider changes in society. Actions speak louder than words, and we keep pushing forward to reach the IKEA ambition for 2013 – to become a circular and climate positive business and to offer healthier

and more sustainable solutions at scale that more and more people can afford.

(Jesper Brodin, President and CEO, Ingka Group)

The CEO of Ingka Group, Mr. Jesper Brodin further continues in the Annual Summary & Sustainability report for 2019, that he aims to simply create 'a new IKEA in three years'. 2019 was the first year of this advantageous journey.

The 3-year transformation of IKEA touches virtually every single part of the company. This strategy almost follows the doctrine that not a single stone may be left unturned. The ten tasks are meant to enable the company to anticipate what might become fundamental changes in customer behaviour and expectations.

The three-year target reflects one fundamental requirement in global business. The speed to adapt to changing circumstances. 'Whether it's where and how people shop their furniture, how they get it home or the environmental impact of our business, our customers' expectations are changing fast, and so will we' makes IKEA's ambition apparent. The company extends its value chain beyond the two dimensions of range and supply. Speed is where IKEA sees itself as most susceptible. And speed in responsiveness will most likely become a pivotal element in IKEA's integrated corporate strategy. The company summarizes the range of necessary changes as follows:

> As we transform Ingka Group to be a more digital, connected and innovative retailer, we all need to change how we work and adopt new ways of doing things.
>
> (INGKA Group – Annual Summary & Sustainability Report FY 2019)

A more detailed overview of IKEA's current scope of activities is provided by the holding company INGKA. As such, the company separates its strategic investment fields into three areas that are expected to play a crucial role in the company's transformation into a global technology-based production and service firm.

The investment branch of INGKA holds a broad variety of shareholdings in a number or areas that are aimed to support the development of IKEA towards new technology areas. As such, the company states its view on the expected scope and contribution of its investment activities to bolster its 3-year transformation strategy:

> With minority and majority shareholding investments, we continue to focus even more on investments in prioritized areas that support our retail business. We're ramping up investments and acquisitions in retail tech, including digital, customer fulfilment, sustainability and a range of services including logistics and delivery services.

The overview of strategic investment areas shows three key focus points emphasized by the company.

The first area relates to investments that are meant to create and increase a more sustainable footprint and waste reduction through the operational production chain of IKEA; coined 'Circular IKEA'. In 2019 alone, IKEA already generated the equivalent to 93% of energy used in the company's operation, up from 81% in 2018 as the report shows. On their long-term strategy, IKEA aims to become a zero-waste and circular company powered with 100% renewable energy in 2030.

Second, 'Retail and Services' is meant to cater to changing customer demands by investing in interior robotics solutions and software platforms for home furnishing and renovation. One relevant area is IKEA's effort to reduce emissions through its operation, delivery and customer travel. This is done by developing electrical charging stations for customer vehicles and offering full electric or emission-free delivery by 2025.

The third area, 'Digitalization and Innovation' incorporates a broad range of technological areas such as plant-based food developments and investments in smart logistic service providers. This investment area shows again the two-sided approach of IKEA. Based on a legacy of self-assembled furniture, logistics and convenience food, the company sets sail in new but related directions.

As such, INGKA's investment areas reflect two aspects. First, it shows the alignment with the historical legacy of IKEA's core area of home furnishing for retail customers across the globe. Second, it displays the organizational choices already undertaken by the company to translate its strategic ambition into practical steps. Hence, the target timeline for the reformulation of a new adaptable business model is set at three years. To quickly enable the company to achieve a new way of sustainable growth, both its strategic investments as well as the changes to its ongoing business activities require fast results. This illustrates that range, supply and timeliness are pivotal elements in the reformulation of a sustainable innovation agenda.

The scale of operations that take place at INGKA Group illustrates the role it plays both directly within the realm of its business as well as indirectly through its network of suppliers, intermediaries and service facilitators.

> We want to use our scale as a buyer to influence standards in our supply chain, selecting suppliers who share our values and work together to have a positive impact on societies and communities. We expect our suppliers to treat their co-workers fairly and to adopt the IKEA supplier code of conduct.
>
> (INGKA Group – Annual Summary &
> Sustainability Report FY 2019)

One element of the company's code of conduct – called the IKEA Way on Purchasing Products, Materials and Services, IWAY – comprises a detailed risk assessment of each individual supplier together with risk mitigation measures.

IWAY represents two sides of the same coin. On the one side, it provides insights into the way the company aims to manage the extensive network of suppliers by creating commitment with IKEA's value base. On the other side, it provides the company with a tool for taking a risk-based view on its supplier network. And more important, the company is now able to evaluate ways to mitigate the risks entailed in its global chain of operations before they become imminent. Again, timeliness in responses is a clear element in IKEA's business strategy.

The case of IKEA shows how important a shared set of norms and values is to formulate a comprehensive risk governance framework. Mr. Justo Candel, who works as IWAY Sustainability Developer for INGKA and who is cited in the Annual Summary & Sustainability Report 2019, states that 'there's a real sense that we'll face challenges together and work with our suppliers to find solutions'. Hence, INGKA is able to realize benefits from established supplier relationships by simultaneously improving the company's business strategy sustainably. Mr. Candel continues, that 'as IWAY experts, we share our knowledge with our suppliers to help them maintain compliance. We have strict requirements, but that doesn't mean we're forcing them to spend a lot of time or money on unnecessary processes'. This statement indicates a few elements that are relevant to the company. First, knowledge about compliance issues is not kept locked away. Severe compliance issues are brought to the attention of all people engaged 'to share learnings across the company'. Second, a risk-based approach of the IWAY code of conduct is thoroughly based on a framework of 'internal and external data to assess risks based on the suppliers' location and the individual characteristics of the business they run'. As such, risk and reward are still considered as two sides of the same coin.

Making IKEA ready for the upcoming changes in consumer behaviour and living circumstances is a major challenge to the company. As such, one might have to imagine a future in which IKEA is not associated with BILLY bookcases, Småland and kødbollar meatballs any more. Instead, how about bug-meatballs, zero-waste sofas and receiving your furniture delivered at home by fully electric vehicles?

Pointers to strategic conversation

1. In what way have IKEA's international operations contributed to its competitive success?
2. Companies often extend their reach incrementally. Why do they pursue this approach?
3. Did IKEA pursue an incremental approach to internationalization?
4. Which resources and capabilities of IKEA have facilitated its international expansion?

Sources

¹ IKEA company website: www.ikea.com

² Forbes Magazine – The Digital Transformation to Keep IKEA Relevant: Virtual Reality, Apps and Self-Driving Cars (19 October 2018): www.forbes.com/sites/bernardmarr/2018/10/19/the-amazing-digital-transformation-of-ikea-virtual-reality-apps-self-driving-cars/#382b67b376be

³ IKEA Range & Supply – company website: https://inter.ikea.com/en/inter-ikea-group/ikea-range-and-supply/

⁴ INGKA Group – Annual Summary & Sustainability Report FY 2019: www.ingka.com/wp-content/uploads/2020/01/Annual-Summary-Sustainability-Report-FY19.pdf

Conclusion

This chapter has highlighted the importance of a firm's reach which is the extent of its international operations. Extended reach provides access to key resources and capabilities which are one of the sources of competitive advantage. We have identified the key ingredients of competitive success at a specific foreign location, and they are: firm-specific advantages, home country-specific advantages and host country conditions. The transnational company has become the dominant organizational form in international business. Its success can be explained by its key ability – the capability to combine immobile resources that are specific to a location, with mobile resources which can be transferred at ease across national borders. However, extending reach and going global gives rise to specific challenges which firms need to overcome in order to become transnational.

Notes

1 See Zaheer, 1995, for an empirical investigation of the idea.
2 See Bartlett and Ghoshal (2000).
3 The Stage Model of Internationalization originated from the classic paper authored by Johanson and Vahlne in 1977. It is also referred to as the Uppsala Model. Jan Johanson, one of the co-authors of the paper, was a professor of International Business in Uppsala University at the time.
4 See Ghemawat (2007).
5 For more information on the Born-Global firms, please refer to the following website of London Business School: www.london.edu/think/born–global.
6 For a detailed exposition of the idea of 'Born Globals' see Oviatt and McDougal, 1994.
7 For a good overview of the complexities that are specific to international operations, see Bartlett and Ghoshal, 2002.
8 More information on the acquisition of Jaguar Land Rover by Tata Motors, can be found on the company website: https://media.jaguar.com/node/9502.

9 The generic model presented here is derived from Dunning's OLI model (see Dunning, 2000). The crucial difference between our model and Dunning's is that we make the distinction between firm-specific advantages and home country-specific advantages whereas Dunning subsumed the latter within the former. We also highlight the host country conditions as a generic success factor for competitive success (and not limited to foreign production as detailed in the OLI model).

Further reading

Bartlett, C. A., & Ghoshal, S. (2000). Going global: Lessons from late movers. *Harvard business review, 78*(2), 132–142.

Bartlett, C. A., & Ghoshal, S. (2002). *Managing across borders: The transnational solution.* Boston, MA: Harvard Business Press.

Dunning, J. H. (2000). The eclectic paradigm as an envelope for economic and business theories of MNE activity. *International business review, 9*(2), 163–190.

Ghemawat, P. (2007). *Redefining global strategy: Crossing borders in a world where differences still matter.* Boston, MA: Harvard Business Press.

Hannah, L. (1996). Multinationality: Size of firm, size of country, and history dependence. *Business and economic history, 25*(2), 144–154.

Johanson, J., & Vahlne, J. E. (1977). The internationalization process of the firm: a model of knowledge development and increasing foreign market commitments. *Journal of international business studies, 8*(1), 23–32.

Johanson, J., & Vahlne, J. E. (2009). The Uppsala internationalization process model revisited: From liability of foreignness to liability of outsidership. *Journal of international business studies, 40*(9), 1411–1431.

Oviatt, B. M., & McDougall, P. P. (1994). Toward a theory of international new ventures. *Journal of international business studies, 25*(1), 45–64.

Zaheer, S. (1995). Overcoming the liability of foreignness. *Academy of Management journal, 38*(2), 341–363.

6

ROOTS

Power of the place

Among the four Rs – Resources, Recombination, Reach and Roots – that underpin competitive advantage, Roots may well be the most underappreciated as a success factor. We take our roots for granted. We attribute our personal success to our intelligence, not to our family, community and nation. We forget that while individual intelligence is evenly distributed across the globe, income inequality between countries is extreme. We do not pay attention to the fact that most creative activities originate in cities. We ignore that world class companies often congregate together in small physical spaces. The strategic management literature has a lot to say about how firms should position themselves within the industry, but surprisingly little about *where* to physically locate themselves. Sometimes for the firm, the industry in which it is currently competing is only transitory while the location is permanent.[1] But, in the current digital age hasn't 'place' lost its relevance? If you can both serve your customer and provide your services remotely, then what is the significance of your physical location? A lot, we argue later in this chapter.

Conventional strategy texts do not take 'place' seriously. The closest they get to acknowledging any role of place in the generation of competitive advantage is in the discussion around the home national environment. The concept of 'roots' that we are putting forward here is multidimensional which encompasses the nation, a spatial region, city and the community.

Importance of roots

Where do you want to put your roots down? When someone asks you the question, they want to know where you intend to settle down permanently. The same goes for companies. They can either choose to have their roots in their home nation or in another country. A lot depends on that decision.

The area of Silicon Valley is about 122 square kilometres (47 square miles). If Silicon Valley were a country, its GDP would be around US$275 billion with a per capita GDP of around $128,000. It has produced many of the top multinational companies in the world including Apple, Google and HP, for example. London is much bigger than Silicon Valley at 1,600 square kilometres (607 square miles), but it makes an even bigger impact on the nation's GDP than Silicon Valley. London produces 22% of UK GDP despite accounting for only 12.5% of the UK population. If you think that this is a twenty first century phenomenon, think again. Fifteenth century Florence was around 104 square kilometres (40 square miles) and a fountain of innovation in painting, sculpture, architecture and commerce. The Renaissance was born in Florence. Creativity and innovation occur in clusters. Geniuses seem to congregate in cities.[2]

Firms can have multiple and mutually non-exclusive roots (see Figure 6.1). Just as an individual can be a Hindu, a New Yorker, and an American simultaneously, firms can have their roots in a community, a city or a region and a nation-state at the same time.[3] Moreover, each of these roots influences firm behaviour, just as our multiple individual identities impact our personal actions.

The conventional strategic management literature has been reluctant to highlight the 'place' as a key success factor. However, one form of 'roots' that they have acknowledged is the nation-state, so let's start with the impact of the nation-state on the competitive advantage of individual firms

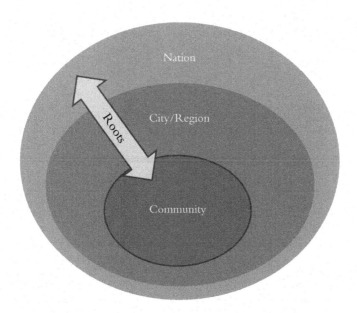

FIGURE 6.1 Multiplicity of roots

Impact of the nation-state

Nation-states are containers of institutions, the rules of the game, factors of production, cultural norms and practices. We are authoring this book in the midst of the Covid-19 pandemic and a search for a vaccine is currently ongoing at a breakneck speed. But medical research on the vaccine is not equally spread over the globe; it is concentrated in a few nations, and within those nations at specific locations. The bioscience cluster in Oxford, UK is one such location. The UK has a **national competitive advantage** in the global pharmaceutical industry. It hosts some of the biggest pharmaceutical companies of the world, including GlaxoSmithKline and AstraZeneca. Similarly, if you look at the global automotive industry, the key manufacturers are based in a few countries – comprising Japan, Korea, USA and Germany. The world is not flat, it is extremely uneven, and it is the impact of the nation-state that causes this unevenness.

The Diamond Model provides an explanatory framework for the competitive advantage of nations (see Figure 6.2).[4]

The Diamond Model is based on four main factors and two peripheral ones. The main factors are:

a. Firm strategy, structure and rivalry
b. Basic and advanced factors
c. Related and supporting industries – clusters
d. Home demand

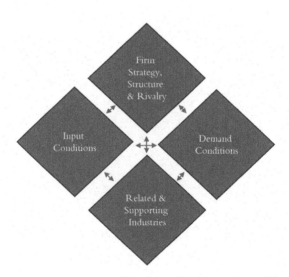

FIGURE 6.2 The Diamond Model

The peripheral factors as per the model are:

a. Chance
b. Government interventions

The Diamond Model incorporates several insights from strategic management, industrial organization, economic geography and international economics. It is a useful model, but it works better as a conceptual framework than as a theory. We will come to this issue later in the chapter but first let us unpack each of the abovementioned factors.

Firm strategy, structure and rivalry

The Diamond Model places great emphasis on the importance of competitive rivalry within the home market. A high level of competitive rivalry makes individual firms perform better. They must differentiate their products more in relation to their competitors or achieve a lower cost structure than their competitors to survive and in the process of competing against one another, they raise the bar and the overall performance of the industry goes up.

The industry structure essentially relates to the level of competition within a particular market, with a **monopoly** situation at one end of the continuum and **perfect competition** at the other. Most products and services that we consume in our daily lives, the bread at the breakfast, the café at the corner of the street for a daily Americano to go, the vehicle that we drive, the computer on which this book is being written, fall under two industry structures: **oligopolistic** and **monopolistic** competitions.[5]

Industries differ from one another on the basis of:

a. Number of competitors
b. Barriers to entry and exit
c. Nature of products, either being differentiated or homogeneous
d. Players have pricing power

The key attributes of oligopolistic competition or an oligopoly are few competitors, significant barriers to entry and exit, and differentiated products, all with some exceptions, and intense non-price competition on, for example, advertisements, marketing and packaging. Firms in an oligopoly usually have some pricing power; that is, they can set their own prices for their products and services. Apple has considerable pricing power. Your local grocer selling vegetables has very little. The automotive industry is an oligopoly, so is the smartphone market. A **duopoly** is a special case of oligopolistic competition, where there are only two players within a given industry. The global aircraft industry for example, is dominated by Airbus and Boeing: a duopoly.

The key attributes of monopolistic competition are many competitors, relatively low barriers to entry and exit, largely homogeneous products but perception of differentiation built through marketing and advertisement spending, and sellers usually do not have any significant pricing power. Your local café faces monopolistic competition as a player in the café industry. A branded sliced bread is another example of monopolistic competition. Important to note here is that monopolistic and monopoly competitions are not the same. In fact, they are very different. Monopoly is a market structure where there is only one player, a situation that arises out of very significant barriers to entry. In most instances, monopolies arise because of government mandates. Government can say that there will be only one water supplier in the country because water is a 'natural monopoly'. In rare cases, a competitive market can also evolve into a monopoly. The market for laptop and desktop computer operating systems is a monopoly, with one player, Microsoft, having close to 90% market share.

Most of the strategic management theories are applicable in markets with oligopolistic competition. Strategy, structure and competitive rivalry are interdependent. The three influence each other in a myriad of ways.

Basic and advanced factors

Here the Diamond Model incorporates insights from international economics. At a general level, the factors of production are land, labour, capital and technology. These factors of production are unevenly distributed across nation-states. This fact is at the base of all international trade.

Conventional theories on international trade are based on the differences that exist among countries in relation to their factors of production. The factors of production in Scotland – its geography and skilled labour – favour the making of Scotch whisky. The factors of production in France favour the making of wine. The theories of absolute and comparative advantage show that both Scotland and France would benefit from specialization. Scotland should produce more Scotch than they can consume, which they do, and France should produce more wine than they can consume, which again they do, and they can trade the surplus with each other, which they also do and both countries will be better off – citizens of both countries can buy more Scotch and wine in this way, rather than trying to produce both commodities in each country without any specialization.

Basic Factors are the resources that nature has endowed to the nation – its geographic location, the minerals, oil and gas that are to be found within its national borders, as well as its (unskilled) labour force. Basic factors can explain international trade in commodities, it can explain why New Zealand has a thriving lamb export business, but it cannot explain the competitive advantage that Germany enjoys in the global automotive industry. To explain that, we need to refer to **Advanced Factors.** While nations are *naturally endowed* with basic factors, they *create* advanced factors. The rule of law is not a gift of nature; it is a human creation. However, the specificities of the rule of law and its enforcement differ from country to country.

Examples of other advanced factors are the country's road and digital infrastructure, its education system, its network of scientific institutions, the list goes on. Advanced factors are essential for manufactured goods and specialized services, particularly those that need a high level of R&D.

Which of these factors, Basic and Advanced, are more important? The data show that developed countries tend to specialize in manufactured goods and services, while developing countries concentrate on the production of commodities. Commodity production depends on basic factors[6] while manufacturing typically needs advanced factors. From this, it is not hard to deduce that advanced factors are critical to the long-term development of the economy. The core–periphery structure of global business is a well-established phenomenon. Core countries specialize in production and export of manufactured goods, while periphery countries export commodities to core countries and import manufactured goods from them. One of the main developmental goals of the periphery countries is industrialization which would ultimately lead to their transformation into one of the core countries. Only a handful of countries have successfully made the transition from periphery to core, Japan and South Korea are the prominent examples. It is instructive to note that these countries have also made huge investments in the development of advanced factors over the years.

Related and supporting industries (clusters)

Firms rarely flourish on their own. Silicon Valley hosts many of the world's top IT firms. This is not an accident. The success of Silicon Valley is linked to the innovation ecosystem that exists in the region. The innovation ecosystem comprises firms, venture capitalists, universities and other scientific institutions. The software giants like Google and Apple that are based in the region benefit from the rest of the ecosystem – graduates from Berkeley and Stanford, new inventions in these universities, and of course the availability of risk capital.[7] Clusters are everywhere. Creative industries in the UK cluster together in London, IT firms in India locate themselves in Bangalore, wine merchants in France try to get a foothold in Bordeaux.

So, what are clusters? They are interconnections of companies and institutions at specific geographical locations. They boost industrial productivity and foster innovation, and in the process enhance the national competitive advantage in specific industries. Clusters excel in competition and collaboration. Firms within a cluster are often competitors but they often collaborate, for example, to increase the market size of their products by converging on a 'dominant design' (see again, Chapter 4).

Home demand

Home demand plays an important role in building competitive advantage of the firm. Home demand is relevant because all firms, barring just a few exceptions, start local. Local or national demand obviously affects firms in a profound way. The size of the home demand is important but so is the quality of that demand. Discerning customers pressurize firms to improve the quality of their products. Japanese customers want the latest state-of-the-art digital cameras and this puts pressure on the Japanese camera manufacturers to improve the quality and features of their products. Imagine that your home country customers are the most discerning lot in the world. If you are then able to satisfy their needs, you are effectively in a position to serve your global customers as well, as they are not going to be as demanding as your home country consumers.

The Diamond is mutually reinforcing. So, home demand motivates firms to up their game, and their higher performance further augments the home demand. The presence of advanced factors facilitates the formation of clusters which in turn affects the development of advanced factors in a positive way.

Now, let us come to the so-called 'peripheral factors' of the Diamond Model. First, there is '**chance**'. Accidents happen. Chance events can dramatically affect, positively or adversely, the fortunes of specific industries. The Covid-19 pandemic dramatically affected the entire landscape, but it is not a gloom story all around. While the hospitality industry suffered, web-conferencing services zoomed up. Car manufacturing ground to halt, but supermarkets registered record sales. Can such chance events profoundly affect national competitive advantage? The answer is, yes. What is the origin story of Silicon Valley in the United States? Following the Second World War which saw increased public investment into military research, the USA and the erstwhile Soviet Union went straight into the Cold War, accelerating government funding of university research in the United States. Spinouts from this university research kickstarted the Silicon Valley revolution. But of course, from a policymaking point of view, chance events are accidents that just happen, and one cannot plan for them. And this brings us neatly to the role of the government within the Diamond Model.

Government impacts all four main pillars of the Diamond. One could be forgiven for thinking that this fact should propel the government to be a main pillar of the Diamond rather than a peripheral one. The treatment of the **role of the government** is one of the main weaknesses of the Diamond Model; we discuss this in detail later in the section. The most direct way that the government can affect national competitive advantage is by developing the country's advanced factors – the higher education system, the road infrastructure, the communication network, the scientific institutions. Its impact on the other pillars of the Diamond are less obvious but nevertheless significant. Government can affect the industry structure and dynamics by its competition policies. It can encourage the formation of regional clusters by providing incentives. Government can also influence home demand through fiscal and monetary policies.

Critiques of the Diamond Model

There are two main drawbacks of the Diamond Model that are worth noting. First, the Diamond Model is a snapshot of an industry at a single point in time within a specific national environment. It is a static analysis. Consider the Japanese automotive

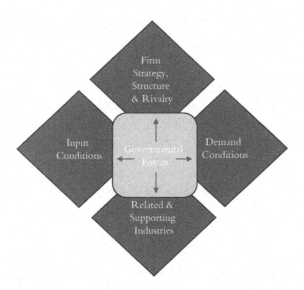

FIGURE 6.3 The role of governmental forces

industry. If you carry out a Diamond Analysis of the industry as it was in the 1960s, you will find that the four pillars of the Diamond were missing-in-action. There was not much home demand for cars, clusters were non-existent, advanced factors were not abundant as yet, and competitive rivalry between domestic car companies not particularly great. Fast forward to 2020 and all four factors are discernible in the Japanese automotive industry. The national competitive advantage of the Japanese automotive industry was built on the back of the export-oriented industrialization strategy of the Japanese Government in the 1960s.[8] And this brings us to the second major critique of the Diamond model – its treatment of the role of the government. Governments play a powerful role in building national competitive advantage. Even within the Diamond Model, it is acknowledged that the government can influence all four main pillars of the Diamond. So, it is quite a puzzle why the model relegates government to only a peripheral role. We can adapt the Diamond Model by putting the governmental force in the middle of the framework, orchestrating the other four pillars (see Figure 6.3).

Creative cities

If the world is indeed flat, as some hyperglobalists claim, then place is not a determinant of success. It does not matter where your roots are, because you have the same level playing field as anyone else across the globe. But if the world is 'spiky' then place matters; your roots matter. The chasm that exists between developed and developing countries in terms of national income should alert us to the fact that the world is indeed spiky and not flat. The spikes are mainly cities and select regions, troughs are the rest of the world. Metro areas generate 93% of the world's patented inventions.[9] Spikes are where innovations happen, where multinationals put down their roots. If you are located in one of these peaks and interact with people in other peaks, the playing field may indeed seem level to you because similar resources and opportunities are available in these locations, but only if you are blindsided to the vast troughs that exist all over the globe. If you are an investment banker who interacts with clients in New York, London, Frankfurt, Singapore, Hong Kong and Mumbai, the world may seem flat as these cities seem pretty similar to each other, but what escapes your attention is that these cities are very different from other places within their own countries.

Cities and clusters that we discussed in the previous section often overlap. However, the idea of the *creative city* is broader than that of the *economic cluster*. An economic cluster has one primary function which is to produce more efficiently and/or innovate more frequently. The creative city encompasses creativity in art, science and technology.[10] In Chapter 4 on Recombination, we discussed how diversity and density in population leads to more creative acts. Opportunities to recombine different ideas are more frequent within a diverse and dense population.

Why are cities so creative? The problem with the idea of clusters is that it has been conceptualized as an economic entity. This relates to a more general problem with the economic and business literature, that it tends to model economic activities as if they are divorced from the rest of society. There is a unity in creative acts, and often creativity in one domain triggers innovation in another.[11] It is not an accident that the city of London excels simultaneously in the fields of science, art and finance, the same is the case with New York.

One of the most important decisions an entrepreneur-founder must make is the question of roots. Where do you put down your roots? Where do you base your operations? The decision can make or break the firm. Yet, remarkably little is said about the matter of the firm's roots within the strategic management literature. Wherever this is a matter of choice, after all some businesses are specific to a location, the rule of thumb is that you try to position your firm within a city or a cluster. The city facilitates the flow of productive resources.[12] Talented people flock to the city, so recruitment becomes easier. Cities, in general, have better physical and communication infrastructure. Companies that are based in cities have access to new research as scientific institutions and universities are often co-located there. Of course, not all cities are equal. Within the commercial domain, cities often specialize in one specific domain. The city of Oxford in the UK for example, has a vibrant bioscience cluster, so if you are a pharmaceutical company, you would want to locate yourself in the region, perhaps in one of the incubator facilities provided by the two universities based in the city.

Why are cities particularly adept at fostering innovation? Mainly because of the social networks that they help in building. A key idea that we can borrow from social networks literature is the **Strength of Weak Ties**.[13] Our social ties can be broadly classified into two types: strong and weak. Your strong social ties are with those who you meet frequently, socialize with and/or share a deep emotional bonding with. Your family, close friends and colleagues with whom you socialize beyond office time are your strong social ties. Weak social ties are your acquaintances. People you have met at a conference, at a networking event or at a dinner party are your weak social ties. Both have their pros and cons. Strong social ties can foster a sense of solidarity,[14] a feeling of belonging to a community. On the other hand, sociologists have pointed out that if you only have strong social ties, it can be like living in a bubble. The same ideas circulate within the group and much of the information becomes redundant fairly quickly. Weak social ties are great for accessing new information.

It has been found that weak social ties are more useful than strong ones for finding new jobs. If you have weak social ties, you also help to bridge **Structural Holes**.[15] Consider a theoretical island that only has two groups. Each of these groups is 'closed'; that is, all the members within the two share only strong social ties. The two groups are socially isolated from each other so there is a structural hole between them; no information is ever transmitted between the two, and no ideas are ever exchanged. The first group has one good idea about hunting, the second group has a bright idea about the gathering of food. As they are isolated from each other, they are not able to profit from each other's productive insights. Now, let's see what happens when one member from the first group befriends another from the second – immediately, the structural hole is bridged. New information flows into the groups which can be used as it is or be recombined with existing information. The social tie between the two members is 'weak' but its impact is profound. The two members stands to gain individually, their standing within the group increases, they become the 'gatekeepers' to the other group, but crucially the groups, as a whole, benefit from the process.

Cities are particularly adept in bringing together disparate communities together, in fostering lots of 'weak ties', in facilitating recombinatorial acts, and in the process engendering innovation.[16] It is for the reasons explained above that cities have become a favoured location for firms to put down their roots.

In Chapter 2, we talked about the two drivers of uncertainty – global flows and digitization. Many commentators believe that these forces are making place less relevant. They suggest that these forces have made the world 'flat' so the firm can be located anywhere and enjoy the same level of access to markets and resources. We could not disagree more. One of the paradoxes of the Digital Age is that the place has become even more important as a success factor. There is a lot of evidence to back this assertion. If you look at the top software firms in the world, many of them are clustered together in a small physical space within Silicon Valley. If you look at the world of filmmaking, again that is clustered in a few select regions of the globe. Why is the importance of place increasing in this so-called Digital Age? It is not difficult to appreciate the answer to this. The pace of innovation has increased significantly, and innovation, as we have already seen, needs recombination of ideas, resources and capabilities, a process that occurs most optimally when people are in close physical proximity with each other.

The culture of community

Culture is a neglected topic in strategic management texts. Culture affects human behaviour and strategic actions are a form of human behaviour, so this neglect is problematic. We are not talking about high culture here (paintings, drama, etc.) rather culture that we encounter daily. Strategy gurus generally steer clear of culture because it is messy, not amenable to fit neatly into managerial 2 × 2 matrices.[17] We do not make any such attempt here. Culture is an under-researched topic in strategic management and whatever little that is out there is not worth drawing insights from. Here we are merely suggesting that community is a form of roots, and entrepreneurial behaviour is often affected by culture that pervades the community.

Some communities encourage entrepreneurial behaviour, some actively discourage it. Enterprise is celebrated in some communities while it is frowned upon in others. The influence of the community is observable more prominently in small and medium-sized businesses where survival of many such organizations is directly dependent on the support from the community. In the UK, 90% of the South Asian restaurants are run by immigrant entrepreneurs from Bangladesh, 90% of whom are from the Sylhet region in the country. The community is critical in running these enterprises. The same phenomenon occurs in Silicon Valley. A disproportionate number of Silicon Valley entrepreneurs are from Taiwan, and the strength of their roots is a major factor behind their success.[18] In India, many of the top industrialists have their roots in the Marwari community from the state of Rajasthan.[19] We discussed strong and weak social ties in the previous section. Strong social ties build cohesion and community spirit. Social norms can be both enabler and constraint to entrepreneurial behaviour.

Firms can exercise some choice in selecting their roots. Most firms remain primarily located in their home nation, even when they become multinationals. Toyota is still very much a Japanese company even if it now has operations across the globe. Within their home nation, firms can choose the location in which they want to establish their operations. In many instances, they choose specific cities or economic clusters for the benefits they derive from being based in these locations. However, community as a root is different from the rest. Just as we cannot choose our parents, founder-entrepreneurs have little choice in the selection of the community they come from. However, it is still important to understand how the community impacts businesses, and this is particularly true in the case of SMEs.

CASE STUDY 6.1: LONDON AND THE FINANCIAL SECTOR

The accelerating pace of digitization, innovative technology and a widespread adoption of the internet are spawning a global marketplace. This may give rise to the notion that the location of a company is irrelevant in this connected world, as it can conduct business by sourcing from supply chains, assembling resources and reaching its customers from anywhere with an internet connection.

Many management strategists have argued that location is no longer relevant in a digitally heightened world, and that companies are more likely to part with their locational identity or dependence[1] in a borderless world with global supply chains and global competition.

The case illustration below seeks to dispel that line of reasoning and attempts to convince evidentially that the location and economic geography (or 'roots') of a business can be a driver of competitive advantage, even in a globalized marketplace. Though companies can effectively leverage technology and resources to conduct business from anywhere, the use of location to configure resources, derive innovation capabilities and utilize networks can generate significant benefits in the short term as well as in the long term.

Many companies continue to view location as a non-core component of their strategy and assess it as a 'real estate' decision, but a pertinent location strategy can make a meaningful difference to company performance.

Admittedly, locational motives of firms have often been rooted in traditional reasons of trade facilitation like access to transport and proximity to major ports or predicated on resource-based logic like convenience, cost of land, availability of labour, energy security and so on.

There are few geo-locations which consistently outperform others in broad economic output or accumulate specialization in a particular sector or activity[2]. As a result, these locations continually attract new economic inhabitants, investment and talent which generate a snowball effect.

Classic locational motives that were driven by traditional trade are undergoing change. Locational decisions are increasingly being driven by new factors like availability of shared talent pools, cross-sectoral collaboration, networking facilities, environmental sustainability factors and innovation supporting ecosystems. Financial and tax incentives and other benefits offered by locational authorities and local/national governments now also play a major part. Efficient legal systems and the presence of regulatory authorities that police fair business practices are also deciding factors.

However, one aspect in the economics of geography is largely ignored in extant business literature, and that is the influence of legacy; in other words the real 'roots' of a location. This aspect becomes especially meaningful if a location possesses past ascendancy and/or had historical significance in international affairs, global politics or trade.

This point is aptly illustrated below using the City of London as an example.

London is a location that not only boasts vast historic prominence as a global trading and political capital in past centuries, but one that has continually evolved to embrace the new. It has successfully established itself in the top three of global financial centres, as a global news centre and, more recently, one of the top destinations for inward investment in technology and the 'startup economy', especially in financial technology.

London leverages the influence of its deep connections to the world from its Imperial past, aided by its handy central time zone location and non-extreme climate, to forge business and trade deals. It also facilitates deal-making by other nations.

In the next few pages, London is depicted as a successful example of two important location-related economic phenomena in business strategy: Clustering and Agglomeration. Both of these occurrences are known to help drive sustainable competitive advantage for the location that manifests them but also for all the firms nested in it.

A business cluster[3] is a geographical concentration of interconnected companies, specialized suppliers, service providers, firms in related industries and associated institutions (e.g. universities, standards institutions, trade associations) in a particular field, which compete but also cooperate. Clusters are considered to increase the productivity with which companies can compete nationally and globally.

The incidence of clustering, in and around cities has several well-known historical illustrations: for example, Flemish cloth in the Flanders area of Belgium in the twelfth century, Bordeaux in France for wineries in the fifteenth century, North West England for textile mills during the Industrial Revolution, and more recently, Hollywood, Detroit and Silicon Valley in the USA for film making, car-making and computer technology, respectively.

One of the most compelling examples in the world that has achieved prominence as an enduring and thriving cluster is the City of London. The 'city in a city' stands as a pivotal international banking hub. Companies that constitute the different segments of the financial sector like banks, brokerage houses, insurance, exchanges, trading desks, market makers and investment banks among others, all benefit from the talent, infrastructure and connections in the cluster.

The recent emergence of the country's largest financial technology, or Fintech, cluster at the 'Silicon roundabout' in the eastern fringes of the City is another example of location as a strategic constituent of competitive advantage. This fintech cluster has a symbiotic but mutually enriching relationship with the 'City's' finance cluster. The flow of resources, capital and talent between these two clusters have assisted both of them to innovate, grow and thrive. Consequentially, London – and the UK – has forged its place as the fintech capital of Europe.[7]

The 'roots' or the historical precedents of London as a nucleus of international trade has contributed a big part in these achievements.

London was established after the Roman invasion of AD 43 as a port city on the Thames River, at its lowest practicable point of crossing. Seafaring ships could load and unload freight and a bridge was built to allow people movement and navigation. The flat topography of the surrounding land and a relatively moderate climate added to its attraction for inland trade. It soon became a thriving nucleus of trade and commerce with Europe and the world.

Over the centuries, London became a magnet to attract trade merchants, entrepreneurs and money lenders, as well as migrants from across the Roman Empire, Europe, Middle East, Africa and Asia.

London started to develop as one of the world's most important cities of that era which in turn facilitated its early origins as a leading financial centre in the 'Square Mile' as it is known today.

The Royal Exchange was built in 1565 as a commercial hub in London as new kinds of stockholding companies were formed and trading mushroomed in new types of goods and commodities from colonies in the New World.

The merchants and money lenders in the City formed associations to fuel this economic expansion, but it was the burgeoning trade with India and Asia, and the Atlantic trade with North America and the Caribbean that really created a need for financing which surpassed the capability of private merchants and financiers.

In 1694, the Bank of England was established as a joint stock company to purchase government debt. Its primary purpose was to act as the nation's financier to fund the military in the nine-year war with France. However, over the next few decades, it endowed huge benefits to the economy by transforming the older gold-standard currency system to a contemporary credit-based market-driven financial system that would serve as a foundation for the growth of the British empire in which 'the sun never set'.

In addition to shipping and trade financing, progress started to occur in the banking and credit sector. Several new financial instruments were created – many of them being the early variants of those in use, even today.

As the seat of the British government, the Crown and the Church, London's position gradually escalated into the pivotal nub of British politics, trade and banking. It attracted capital flows domestically as well as internationally.

Continuing that tradition, London remains a pre-eminent 'headquarters City' for several global banks as well as a host to nearly every global financial institution. Its reputation became pronounced in the eighteenth century as a top global choice for business, finance and banking, which continues today. London ranks second, after New York, in the Global Financial Centres Index (26 March 2020)[6] in a ranking of the competitiveness of financial hub cities worldwide.

The expansion and reach of British colonies in the eighteenth, nineteenth and early twentieth centuries generated prosperity and an enduring economic expansion in Britain. It was accompanied by the Industrial Revolution. The resulting transformations in the economy created a need for reliable banking, credit and savings for both businesses and people.

London nurtured a domestic money market in the early nineteenth century which drew financial interest from banks at home and across its colonies. An increasing requirement for finance to fuel domestic economic growth implored British banks to look overseas. This marked the beginnings of international banking arrangements that have developed into modern correspondent banking as we know today.

The inflow and repatriation of capital, money and investments across business and people in its colonies gave rise to the formation of international payment mechanisms, propelling London to become a top international banking centre in the world, a position that it enjoys even today.

Innovations like these were the genesis of a progressive financial sector in London that have actuated it to claim a leading place in several financial products over the years. In fact, London was instrumental in developing the foreign exchange market and creating new financial products such as the Eurodollar, a hybrid between foreign exchange and the Eurobond market. London was a pre-eminent player in the Eurodollar market when it developed in the 1950s after the Second World War. More recently, London has evolved into a leader and multi-trillion-dollar global hub for financial derivatives.

Lloyds of London, formed in 1686 originally for marine insurance remains one of the top marketplaces in the world for insurance and re-insurance, and has played a pivotal role in the growth of the insurance and underwriting industry globally.

Fast forward to the current decade and London continues to lead in contemporary financial products as a thriving hub for foreign exchange, bonds and their futures. After nearly 500 years, several wars and the extinguishing of the British colonial empire, London continues to maintain its pole position in the world's financial economy and hosts over 500 banks, including 251 foreign banks.[9]

London's colonial past has created extensive networks with banks all over the world that access financial 'market makers' in London. As a result, London is the global forerunner with 43% share[10] of the $6.6 trillion-a-day market [11] in foreign exchange transactions.

The list goes on. The London bullion exchange is by far the largest global centre for over-the-counter bulk trading in bullion gold and silver, and metal markets, through the historic London Bullion and London Metal Exchanges.

In the last few decades, several cities have been emerging as global financial centres including Singapore, Beijing and Frankfurt, and they may even harbour ambitions to displace London's pre-eminence as a world financial hub; but London enjoys an invisible and unique strength.

London's 'roots' are unassailable.

It was the capital of the British Empire, which at its pinnacle, was the foremost global power. By 1913, the British Empire held sway over 412 million people, 23% of the world's population at the time and covered 24% of the Earth's total land area.[12]

For more than five centuries, that latitude served to proliferate a far-reaching political, legal, linguistic and cultural influence which remains a legacy in most continents. Numerous post-colonial economies, including America, have based their financial, legal and commercial systems on the English systems, in varying proportions. English commercial law continues to be adopted for the majority of international finance transactions.

This historical precedence has bred familiarity and confidence, and, to date, is a significant factor in attracting foreign companies and investments to the UK. The first stop of such investment and economic talent is usually London because of its position as the most diverse region in the country. Forty per cent of London residents identify as Asian, Black, Mixed or other ethnic groups.[13]

Familiar English language, an equitable legal system, a forward-looking market regulator and transparent international business practices attract foreign financial institutions. An enduring and well-entrenched commercial environment bolsters that motivation, supported by the city's strong trading networks and financiers from its colonial merchant era.

As a result, London powers the biggest industry in the country – banking and financial services – and propels the UK to be the world's largest net exporter of financial services. In 2018, the financial services sector was the largest single sector at 6.9% of total economic output that generated 1.1 million or 3.1% of all UK jobs, £29 billion in tax and £132 billion to the UK economy.[14]

London's contribution was £63.8 billion or nearly half of the national output in banking and financial services. Little surprise that the sector constitutes 15% of London's total economic output. [15]

As a result of its historical roots, the UK has also consistently been the number one location for foreign direct investment in financial services over the last twenty years. In 2019, it led with more than twice the number of financial services projects registered than in Germany in second place.[16] That leadership has also cemented London's position as a leading global centre for financial technology inward investment.

London's population has reflected and, indeed, fuelled that economic growth. It rose from approximately 50,000 in the early 1500s to a million by the late eighteenth century. In this century, from 2000 onwards, it has been growing steadily at 1.4% average.

The international complexion of its growing population over the years infused an assortment of business and societal pursuits, while its centuries-old history of trade in a multitude of goods has shaped the city to gradually evolve into a cluster of clusters.[5]

The growth of the dominant financial sector has boosted growth and investment in common resources such as underground railways, roads, buildings, skilled labour in support services, restaurants and entertainment. London's business roots have created positive externalities that have developed and grown several different industries.

These include news companies centred on Fleet Street, jewellery at Hatton Garden, Fintech on Old Street, bespoke tailoring on Savile Row, music and fashion in Soho, theatre and media companies in the West End and premium brand retailing on Regent Street among others.

These varied business clusters are bound by a common theme – a heritage born out of a diversified portfolio of a trading nation. The resultant elements of people, capital, business and knowledge, supported by strategic economic vision and developmental agencies have, over time, ushered London into becoming a city with an undeniable competitive advantage. London today exemplifies the urbanization economies of agglomeration, as introduced in Alfred Marshall's 'Principles of Economics' of 1920.[17]

In extant discourse on business strategy, it is mentioned that cost of capital, labour, profits and efficiency (i.e. classical demand and supply factors) lead to competitive advantage. That may include locational decisions. For example, marine processing plants are usually located close to sea-ports, or steel plants are in proximity to iron ore mines.

Over the last two decades, E-commerce and internet enablement have facilitated firms to reach customers and access marketplaces formerly unavailable, and, hence, it was only supply side factors that were impacted by a locational decision.

In the emerging digital economy and knowledge society we live in today, supply chains have also started to evolve. Firms must persistently search for ways to leverage resources to generate competitive advantage, and, as the example of London manifests above, a location strategy that leverages the 'roots' or the history of economic geography can be critical, even key to discovering competitive advantage.

Pointers for strategic conversation

1. Has London's importance as a business hub increased or decreased with the advent of globalization and digitization?
2. How important is it for firms to be located within a cluster?
3. How has the digitization of the global economy affected the choice of location for firms?

Sources

[1] The role of location in competition – Michael E. Porter, (Porter, 1994; Pinch et al., 2003).
[2] *The Competitive Advantage of Nations*, Michael E. Porter 1990.
[3] Wikipedia: Business Cluster https://en.wikipedia.org/wiki/Business_cluster
[4] www.centreforlondon.org/blog/why-businesses-cluster-in-london/
[5] www.pearl-coutts.co.uk/the-insider/resources/types-of-business-clusters-in-london
[6] GFCI 27 Report by Z/Yen Partners and China Development Institute, March 2020.
[7] Investopedia: How London became the world's financial Hub. Deborah Dsouza www.investopedia.com/how-london-became-the-world-s-financial-hub-4589324

[8] www.thecityuk.com/research/key-facts-about-the-uk-as-an-international-financial-centre-2018/

[9] www.uncsbrp.org/finance.htm

[10] www.cityam.com/uk-lead-in-forex-is-envy-of-world/

[11] www.bloomberg.com/news/articles/2019-09-16/global-currency-trading-surges-to-6-6-trillion-a-day-market

[12] https://en.wikipedia.org/wiki/British_Empire

[13] www.ethnicity-facts-figures.service.gov.uk/uk-population-by-ethnicity/national-and-regional-populations/regional-ethnic-diversity/latest

[14] https://researchbriefings.files.parliament.uk/documents/SN06193/SN06193.pdf

[15] www.ons.gov.uk/economy/grossdomesticproductgdp/bulletins/regionaleconomicactivitybygrossdomesticproductuk/1998to2018/pdf

[16] www.ey.com/en_uk/news/2020/06/uk-retains-top-spot-for-financial-services-investment-in-europe-and-is-expected-to-outperform-the-continent-post-covid-19

[17] https://archive.org/details/in.ernet.dli.2015.149776

CASE STUDY 6.2: THE DIGITAL MEDIA CITY IN SEOUL, SOUTH KOREA

Cities tended to historically separate their crafts. Many city-landscapes are shaped in the present day by their early trade and craft guilds – such as Antwerp with its famous diamond trading district, Boston's Leather District or the many neighbourhoods that reflect migration movements, such as Little Italy, Little Odessa or China Town in New York City.

In times past, the city's council had some say in deciding where certain craft guilds were allowed to settle. Close geographic proximity appears to be of lasting appeal to business-minded people around the globe.

The benefits to its residents appear to more than out-play its shortcomings. Hence, popular urban districts do generally increase competition for scarce resources, such as employees with specialized technological knowledge, valuable rental offices or affordable living places to its residents.

Interestingly enough, it appears that the formation of business clusters actually provides a remedy to competitive forces in a company sector. To join forces within the same geographical location indicates that those companies perceive the advantageous effects to be more valuable than the competitive forces.

Business clusters display a dominant unifying factor that companies share with each other – in Silicon Valley, it's where the technology industry gathers, around Milan in Northern Italy, the fashion industry cluster is settled. These types of orchestrated business agglomerations are genuine policy initiatives of city councils to form a sustainable contribution to its economy.

In Seoul, the capital of South Korea, the Digital Media City (DMC) is an agglomeration of residential and office space for entertainment, media and IT-companies.

DMC is an urban-planning project initiated by the municipal authorities of Seoul. The project is part of the larger Millennium City project in the city district of Sangam-dong in Seoul.

It appears that the city government and public authorities shared the same view on the success of Korea's media and entertainment industry (M&E), when deciding on how to cope with an under-developed city district in early 2000:[1]

> A long-term stabilization plan was decided for the regeneration of the former contaminated area. Its main goal was to restore the environment and to transform the area into an eco-friendly park. The overall objective is to contribute realizing a self-sufficient city that offers pleasant working conditions and advanced IT infrastructure.

As the Metropolitan Authority of Seoul describes the vision behind DMC: 'It will be the world's first planned media & entertainment and IT cluster.'

The idea to re-develop the district of Sangam-dong was first announced in 1999. The Metropolitan Authority of Seoul initiated the project to develop an action plan. This plan was prepared by the Seoul Development Institute, an urban planning facility together with the MIT Graduate School of Urban Studies and Architecture. To ensure that future residents will indeed specialize in the digital M&E industry, the municipal authority classified prospective tenant units into one of three categories: key facilities, recommended facilities and general facilities.

In 2011, the area was 94.5% occupied by residents engaged in the envisioned high-tech M&E industries, the Urban Sustainability Exchange reports the following reasons for its success:

> The municipal government attributes [the occupancy rate of 94.5% of M&E residents] to the following: firstly, geologically [sic; should be geographic] convenient location, secondly, sufficient transport infrastructure; and thirdly, active cooperation between occupant companies and the city's support measures for them.

The majority of companies residing in DMC are rather small. Almost 70% report fewer than 30 employees. As the Urban Sustainability Exchange continues to report, the municipal authorities consider it 'a big achievement that the complex provides many small-sized businesses with fewer than 20 employees with office space, thereby helping to realize the agglomeration economy by utilizing the intra-complex network'.

As such, the effect of intra-complex networks on small companies and startups are a vital reason for Seoul's city government to pursue the DMC project. Those network effects are relevant for consideration. The results of DMC were widely shared with MIT, and covered in international newspapers.

The Korean Wave

The Metropolitan Authority of Seoul does not shy away from aligning its urban structures to global trends.[2]

> DMC will greatly contribute to Korea's positioning in the knowledge-based market of the 21st century through its advanced IT, human resources, and entertainment capabilities as already demonstrated through the global phenomenon dubbed Korean Wave.

One of the most well-known products of the Korean M&E industry is a range of K-pop artists and bands. Who doesn't immediately remember 'Gangnam Style' by PSY raging in 2012? The music clip is YouTube's most watched video clip ever. With more than 2 billion views, the success of the clip required YouTube to alter the maximum view limit to more than 9 quintillion.[20] Apparently, YouTube doesn't expect the success of Gangnam Style to fade away.

As the Metropolitan Authority of Seoul continues to outline, DMC is meant to be used as a laboratory for twenty-first-century urban innovation. With free wireless broadband internet access, the district is able to facilitate instant communication networks among its residents.

> The DMC project is not just a simple urban development plan; it not only deals with the physical development of a new sub-centre of a metropolis but also represents the first attempt to integrate the urban and economic development of Seoul.

The City of Seoul continues ambitiously that 'the future growth of social capital to lay the groundwork for Korea's sustainable development' is aimed for. This aspirational plan is put to work by the joint efforts of an academic-industry-research initiative.

As such, DMC has three roles: first, to develop Seoul into a geopolitical 'centrepiece of East Asia'. The Korean capital aspires to integrate transportation means – through high speed trains, airport and highway – to become the hub for East Asia's air travel.

Second, DMC aims to constantly produce new media content by integrating culture and IT. Hence, DMC 'will be a catalyst of "glocalization" to satisfy the two complementary demands of globalization and localization of culture', the municipal authorities continue.

The third role of DMC is described as 'amplifier of the knowledge industry'. As such, the project aims to connect East Asia with the rest of the world by means of the services its digital media industry delivers.

Regarding the question of how to achieve a world-leading M&E industry in Seoul, DMC outlines two relevant aspects. First is the physical development of the urban area where DMC is situated. As an industrial complex, the business agglomeration is intended to form a melting-pot between future-oriented IT technology and Korea's cultural heritage.

The second aspect relates to the economic development of Seoul. As the Metropolitan Authority describes its ambition:

> DMC is designed to be a hi-tech city of information that will become an international Mecca of all things from the media world to a grand hub of economic, cultural, and eco-friendly developments.

The Metropolitan Authority of Seoul expects to achieve a number of beneficial effects through its DMC initiative. Besides economic benefits, cultural and environmental benefits are equally important.

The concept of a business agglomeration in itself does not stop at the level of the city's district. Potential tenants and companies in the cluster are invited to participate in smaller research groups, and so-called 'mini-clusters' during a forum coined DMC CoNet. Tenant companies receive the opportunity to participate in councils for networking purposes, idea development and cross-fertilization. On a higher level, tenant companies are invited to participate in international conferences to share their experiences and practices with various business parties. As such, the idea to create, facilitate and develop synergies among its tenants is guiding the efforts of the Metropolitan Authorities and its stakeholders.

To be able to sustain its current edge, a number of initiatives have been announced by the Metropolitan Authority of DMC.

A view on the future

DMC initiated a set of three initiatives to ensure a sustainable composition of new and established M&E companies. All three ideas share the view of Seoul's Metropolitan Authority to integrate technology, culture and sustainable development with Korea's ambition to develop and enhance its position as geographical hub in East Asia.

The DMC Hi-Tech Industry Center

The Hi-Tech Industry Center[3] is a developmental initiative to cater to the specific needs and requirements of both established and startup companies in the area of digital media content and software development. As such, the programme provides affordable office space together with the respective broadband infrastructure to facilitate high-tech companies.

Furthermore, the initiative provides an extensive range of governmental and municipal support programmes to facilitate the development of its tenant companies. Those support programmes are intended to enhance the likelihood of companies in the Industry Center to achieve a competitive position.

The DMC Hi-Tech Industry Center initiative is dedicated to prospective tenants across a range of specialities, comprising computer games, animation and mobile technology as well as broadcasting, advertising and other forms of digital content production.

The DMC R&D Center

The second initiative relates to the DMC R&D Center, or as it is fully named, the DMC Business-University Collaboration Research Center.[4]

The R&D Center aims to facilitate research on business strategy, media and entertainment. As such, the Center is meant to lay a sustainable foundation underneath the future ambitions of Seoul as global leader in digital media productions and IT.

Companies that enjoy the benefits of the R&D Center facilities and support, comprise digital media companies, software and IT-development firms as well as university research centres and university spin-offs.

The DMC Gallery

The third initiative illustrates the vital element in Seoul's understanding of how to integrate technology with culture and art. The DMC Gallery provides exhibition areas and facilities to promote digital M&E projects.[5]

The Gallery includes the full scope of facilities to enjoy digital media productions. Hence, it covers a 3D stereoscopic image hall, an experience centre to showcase DMC facilities and numerous exhibition halls. The DMC Gallery constitutes a world-class facility for both its residents and the general public for cultural productions.

Given the various initiatives and support programmes issued, we deem it likely that for the foreseeable future the Korean Wave is here to stay.

Pointers for strategic conversation

1. How important have clusters been to the Korean economic 'miracle'?
2. Do clusters contribute towards the international competitiveness of firms? How?
3. What impact have culture and community had on the competitive success of companies?

Sources

[1] Urban Sustainability Exchange, official website: https://use.metropolis.org/case-studies/sangam-digital-media-city-dmc-city-of-tomorrow

> 2 Seoul Digital Media City, official website of the metropolitan authority – Meaning of DMC: http://seouldmc.kr/cntntsService.do?siteId=SITE_00000000000017&menuId=MNU_0000000000000261
>
> 3 Digital Media City, official website of the metropolitan authority – Facilities in Operation - Hi-Tech Industry Center: http://seouldmc.kr/cntntsService.do?siteId=SITE_00000000000017&menuId=MNU_0000000000000281
>
> 4 Digital Media City, official website of the metropolitan authority – Facilities in Operation – DMC R&D Center: http://seouldmc.kr/cntntsService.do?siteId=SITE_00000000000017&menuId=MNU_0000000000000282
>
> 5 Digital Media City, official website of the metropolitan authority – Facilities in Operation – DMC Gallery: http://seouldmc.kr/cntntsService.do?siteId=SITE_00000000000017&menuId=MNU_0000000000000283

Conclusion

In this chapter we have explored the different forms of roots: nation, city/region and community. Where you are from matters a lot in global business. That is the paradox of competitive success in the twenty-first century. As the business environment has become more globalized and digitized, the place has not diminished in significance, in fact, the opposite has happened. Conventional strategic management literature, in general, has a weak conception of the importance of place or roots, limiting itself to the analysis of national environment. We have shown in this chapter why that approach can be unsatisfactory. The idea of roots needs to be broad enough to encompass additional factors like city, region and community.

Notes

1 Consider Netflix. It has evolved from a mail order company to streaming third-party content over the internet to producing original entertainment content. It has migrated from one industry sector to another while being based in the same location, Silicon Valley. Its place has been a constant, its industry transitory.

2 See Weiner (2016).

3 Multiplicity of identity and root is actually the norm. Very few of us have just one identity or root. Although the extant literature is sparse on multiplicity of root, a lot has been written on the matter of identity. See, for example, Sen, 2007.

4 See Porter (1990).

5 The idea of competition in 'imperfect' markets has a long history which can be traced back to the writings of Joan Robinson in the early 1940s. See Robinson, 1942 as an example.

6 In some cases, abundance of Basic Factors can actually inhibit economic development. 'Resource Curse' is a well-established phenomenon in economics. Some oil rich countries also suffer from a high level of corruption, the economic benefits of oil exports accrue only to a tiny elite, and the vast majority of the population is deprived of them. See Sachs and Warner, 2001, for a good overview of the phenomenon.

7 Klepper, 2010, provides a good exposition of the origins of the semiconductor cluster in Silicon Valley and automotive industry cluster in Detroit.

8 See Johnson (1982).

9 See 'The Spiky World of Innovation', available at www.bloomberg.com/news/articles/ 2012-04-03/the-spiky-world-of-innovation.

10 See Hall (2000).

11 The creative unity that exists between endeavours in art, science and technology has been pointed out by historians like Kranzberg, 1967. It has also been emphasized by philosophers like Tagore, 1922.

12 See Florida (2005).

13 See Granovetter (1973, 1983).

14 See Rost (2011).

15 See Burt (2004).

16 Collaboration and creativity go together; networks of friends and acquaintances are central to creative collaborations. See Farrell, 2003.

17 Some have tried to develop frameworks to classify different cultures (see Hofstede, 1983) but these are generally considered as simplistic and of limited value. The main problem with these frameworks is that it considers the nation as the natural unit of analysis when it comes to culture. A nation is made up of many communities, and cultural practices vary widely across them. The claim that a nation has a homogeneous culture is inherently problematic.

18 See Saxenian (2002).

19 See Timberg (1978).

20 A quintillion is one followed by thirty zeros.

Further reading

Burt, R. S. (2004). Structural holes and good ideas. *American journal of sociology*, *110*(2), 349–399.

Farrell, M. P. (2003). *Collaborative circles: Friendship dynamics and creative work*. Chicago: University of Chicago Press.

Florida, R. (2005). *Cities and the creative class*. New York: Routledge.

Granovetter, M. S. (1973). The strength of weak ties. *American journal of sociology*, 78(6), 1360–1380.

Granovetter, M. (1983). The strength of weak ties: A network theory revisited. *Sociological theory*, 1, 201–233.

Hall, P. (2000). Creative cities and economic development. *Urban studies*, *37*(4), 639–649.

Hofstede, G. (1983). National cultures in four dimensions: A research-based theory of cultural differences among nations. *International studies of management & organization*, *13*(1–2), 46–74.

Johnson, C. (1982). *MITI and the Japanese miracle: The growth of industrial policy, 1925–1975*. California: Stanford University Press.

Klepper, S. (2010). The origin and growth of industry clusters: The making of Silicon Valley and Detroit. *Journal of urban economics*, *67*(1), 15–32.

Kranzberg, M. (1967). The unity of science—technology. *American scientist*, *55*(1), 48–66.

Pinch, S., Henry, N., Jenkins, M., & Tallman, S. (2003). From 'industrial districts' to 'knowledge clusters': a model of knowledge dissemination and competitive advantage in industrial agglomerations. *Journal of economic geography*, 3(4), 373–388.

Porter, M. E. (1990). *The competitive advantage of nations: With a new introduction*. New York: Free Press.

Porter, M. E. (1994). The role of location in competition. *International journal of the economics of business*, 1(1), 35–40.

Robinson, J. (1942). *The economics of imperfect competition*. London: Macmillan & Co.

Rost, K. (2011). The strength of strong ties in the creation of innovation. *Research policy*, 40(4), 588–604.

Sachs, J. D., & Warner, A. M. (2001). The curse of natural resources. *European economic review*, 45(4–6), 827–838.

Saxenian, A. (2002). Transnational communities and the evolution of global production networks: the cases of Taiwan, China and India. *Industry and innovation*, 9(3), 183–202.

Sen, A. (2007). *Identity and violence: The illusion of destiny*. New Delhi: Penguin Books India.

Tagore, R. (1922). *Creative unity*. Delhi: Macmillan.

Timberg, T. A. (1978). *The Marwaris, from traders to industrialists*. Delhi: Vikas.

Weiner, E. (2016). *The geography of genius: A search for the world's most creative places from ancient Athens to Silicon Valley*. New York: Simon and Schuster.

7

CREATING OPTIONS

Harnessing the power of uncertainty

We live in the Age of Disruptive Uncertainty. In Chapter 2, we discussed the two main drivers of this disruptive uncertainty – globalization (we analysed it using the framework of global flows in Chapter 2) and digitization. These drivers have made the macro environment more volatile than ever before. The Covid-19 pandemic has made us realize how interconnected the world has become. The virus spread across the globe with breath-taking speed. The flow of the novel coronavirus mirrored a particular form of global flow, the flow of people across national borders.

Global flows, as discussed in Chapter 2, are flows of goods, services, capital, technology and people. The velocity of these flows within a nation-state depends on the country's **Expeditors** and **Barriers**. The velocity of the flows increases with expeditors and decreases with barriers. A globally connected country has lots of expeditors and few barriers, the Netherlands being a good example. It is important to note that nation-states are not passive recipients of disruptive uncertainty. They *choose* this uncertainty, even without perhaps realizing that they have made this choice. What do we mean by this? The barriers and expeditors of global flows are created at the national level. An EU member country has *chosen* to be part of the European Single Market, its membership being an Expeditor. This increases the velocity of the global flows within the country leading to a higher level of uncertainty. However, this was obviously not the main motivation that led the country to seek EU membership in the first place. Countries have joined the EU because of the positive benefits that accrue to them – access to the largest single market in the world, peace and solidarity. But the EU Single Market also makes these countries more globally connected, more open to global flows thus making the macro environment more uncertain.

Digitization has added to the velocity of global flows. This aspect is not well appreciated, even by seasoned commentators. Some think that globalization and digitization are opposite forces. Digitization can lead to, for example, remote working which reduces the need for people having to cross national borders. But this argument is based on a false premise – that globalization is all about immigration and emigration. It clearly is not. Digitization accelerates the global flow in remote services. When we use Amazon to buy goods even from a local supplier, Amazon takes a cut of the proceeds and that represents an export of services. Web conferencing, search engines, emails, cloud services, these pillars of remote working are all part of the global flows. Digitization intensifies globalization and vice versa, the two are complementary to each other.

The increased velocity of global flows, boosted by digitization, has disrupted the macro environment, making it more uncertain. So, what does this mean for strategic management? A lot, we suggest. For some time now, the strategic management field has been critiqued to be suffering from the malaise of **'hyper-rationality'**. We argue here that many of the frameworks need to be adapted given the current condition of disruptive uncertainty. But, let's first understand what the term hyper-rationality means in the context of strategic management.

The problem of hyper-rationality

Much of the strategic management literature is based on neoclassical economics.[1] This is a strength as well as a weakness of the field. The strong analytical trend that is discernible can be credited, in large measure, to economics. This has led to the generation of lots of useful frameworks, many of which have been discussed in the previous chapters of this book. However, in the process, the field has also been burdened with one of the less salutary aspects of neoclassical economics: the pursuit of abstract theorization at the expense of empirical reality. **Homo economicus**[2] is a creation of neoclassical economics. Homo economicus is a utility maximizing human who is obsessed with self-interest. Homo economicus is an abstraction; real people do not behave the way neoclassical economics suggests they do, yet much of economics and strategic management literature is based on such inaccurate assumptions about human behaviour.

The other big influencer of the field has been '**Taylorism**'. Strategic management as a discipline arguably started with Frederick Winslow Taylor's *Principles of Scientific Management* published in 1919. The book is based on a speech that Taylor gave to the American Society of Mechanical Engineers (he was a past president of the Society). It is not surprising then that Taylor regarded business as an engineering system, and management as the task of optimizing the system. His approach was 'scientific' only to the extent that the recording of time and motion of workers engaged in a task can be considered as such. But strategic management has been traditionally burdened with these two axioms: a) businesses are utility maximizing entities preoccupied primarily with the generation of profits; and b) the main goal of management is to achieve efficiency and predictability in the tasks that the business must perform to deliver their goods and services.

Hyper-rationality in strategic management arises from these axioms. These goals are taken for granted and not questioned, even when their applicability to real business situations is quite limited. Hyper-rationality assumes that managers are almost omniscient. This is also a legacy of Frederick Taylor. The main task of the manager is to plan what the workers need to do to achieve the company's goal, which is simply to maximize profits for shareholders. The managers have all the facts they need, they also know how the future is going to pan out, so they can guide the company safely to the desired destination. Needless to say, the reality is very different. In real life, managers have limited information at their disposal, have only a vague idea about the future, and hence cannot and indeed do not try to optimize the route to the destination ahead. This is in fact what is known as **bounded rationality**, which we discuss in the next section.

Hyper-rationality pushes scholars, practitioners and students to treat the conceptual frameworks of strategic management as universal laws, applicable in all contexts. In reality, the ideas and concepts of strategic management are less like scientific theories and more like 'rules of thumb'. None of the frameworks discussed in this book should be considered as a universal law, they all should be treated as useful heuristics.

Bounded rationality: A dose of realism

As already alluded to, entrepreneurs and managers are not endowed with super intelligence. They have cognitive limitations just like the rest of humankind. They do not have access to all relevant information. They are not clairvoyant; they do not know the future. Bounded rationality is decision making under these conditions. Herbert Simon, who coined the term and received the Nobel Prize in Economics in 1978, suggested that managers do not 'optimize', rather they 'satisfice' by taking actions that satisfy their needs.[3] Bounded rationality embraces heuristics or rules of thumb. Managers act based on what has worked in the past, and not on hyper-rational calculations about the optimum outcome. In conditions of hyper uncertainty, bounded rationality becomes even more prominent. In Chapter 5 (Reach: Going global) we discussed how firms internationalize their operations incrementally, both in terms of the markets they enter and in relation to the modes of entry, the 'stage model' of internationalization. This cautious approach is an outcome of the 'bounded rationality' of managers. This is also sometimes referred to as **Logical Incrementalism**, the trial-and-error approach to strategic management.

Hyper-rationality is an abstraction. Humans are not hyper-rational. Economists engage in these kinds of abstraction to develop mathematical formulae to generalize some principles which may be at the base of some real-world phenomenon. By itself, this is not a problem. The problem arises when some economists and/or strategic thinkers argue that this how humans and organizations *should* behave. In other words, trouble brews when abstract thinking becomes normative, a guide for behaviour in the real world. Bounded rationality, on the other hand, is firmly grounded in the real world. It describes how managers make decisions in real business situations. However, its weakness is that it is not a guide for action. So, whereas hyper-rationality is misused as a normative guide for action, bounded rationality self-consciously avoids putting forward strategic frameworks that can aid decision making. This leaves us with a problem. We are missing a framework for strategic action which is not based on inaccurate assumptions about human behaviour, and this is where **optionality** comes in.

Optionality

Optionality is about having the *right* to do something but not the *obligation*. **Real Options** theory, which is about options on real assets as opposed to financial ones, has merited only a niche area within the strategic management literature, mainly due to the fact that it has preoccupied itself with calculations of the net present value (NPV) of assets. In doing so, it has missed seeing the woods for the trees. The value of optionality is bigger if it is taken as a general approach to strategic decision making.[4]

Options are of course not a free lunch. Buying the right to buy something is usually more expensive than buying that thing outright in case you have to exercise that right. So, if an asset costs you £100 to buy after two months, you can buy the right to buy that asset after two months, say for £10. After two months, you have the right but not the obligation to buy that asset. If you decide to buy it, the total cost for you is £110 (£100 + £10). If you do not purchase the asset, that is, you do not exercise your right, the cost is £10.

Once you get the idea you start seeing options everywhere. To write this book, we have entered a contract with the publisher. We have the right but not the obligation to deliver the manuscript on a future date. If we do not deliver, our sunk costs in this book project in terms of time and effort are lost, which can be considered as the option cost here. Authors often have multiple book projects going on simultaneously and follow through with the one that shows most promise; that is, a market demand over time. Unconsciously, these authors are using the idea of optionality. Each book publishing contract represents a real option for them. Companies use the real option approach without labelling it such. Oil companies buy the right to explore for oil in many locations, but the majority of these locations are ultimately not exploited. These exploration rights are real options. 3M is a company that exemplifies option thinking (see the case study).

Optionality is about using our bounded rationality in a strategic manner. Optionality is about accepting small risks and the associated costs but being open to potential big gains. The rationality in option thinking comes from your ability to spot the big payoffs in the options as they appear and then acting on them. There are essentially two kinds of payoffs: concave and convex.

Concave payoffs give steady returns but the upside here is capped while the downside is not – it can potentially go to zero. If you are a franchisee, you may get a steady return on your investment, but your upside is capped – you cannot expand and build economies of scale, which the franchisor can; the downside is significant, if the franchisor goes out of business, so would you. Franchisees enjoy (or endure, depending on your perspective) a concave payoff. If you are a franchisee,

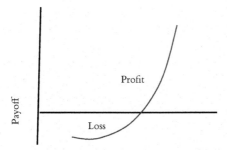

FIGURE 7.1 Convex payoff

you are never going to be the next Google or Microsoft. You may think that there is a trade-off between the steady and 'safe' return of a franchise operation and the uncertainty of a startup, but then you would be the ignoring the inherent concavity of the payoff. Your upside is capped while your downside is potentially open. Franchisees are not entrepreneurs because they are not comfortable with uncertainty.

On the other hand, a company like 3M (see case study) encounters a convex payoff. It experiments with a wide range of products, the majority of which are not particularly successful, but a small handful of products become bestsellers and generate excessive returns. The cost of many experimental product innovations is the option-cost for 3M, the ability to recognize the full potential of some of these products is their bounded rationality, and the return on these products is their **convex payoff** (see Figure 7.1). Entrepreneurial firms are good at identifying businesses with convex payoffs. Entrepreneurial firms embrace uncertainty.

You have to be entrepreneurial to engage with option thinking but not all entrepreneurs think in option terms. Option thinking is based on experimentation; it pursues the trial-and-error approach. Optionality works best in a disruptive environment. When the global flows circulate within the environment in high velocity, the consequences of that become almost impossible to predict. Option thinking comes to the fore in such situations. The interesting thing about uncertainty is that it is Janus-faced, it engenders both risk and reward. The challenge for the organization is to find a strategy that minimizes the risk and maximizes the reward. Maximizing reward involves the search for convex payoffs and avoidance of concave payoffs in real business situations.

Real options and corporate strategy

Corporate strategy is about deciding which business a company should be in. Real options are essentially about diversification into new products, new industries, new markets. If these diversifications make the payoff curve convex for the firm, then they are pursuing the real option approach. Firms have long engaged in diversification of their operations. So, does this mean all diversifications are a form of optionality? We say, no. Real options have the following three attributes:

a. Making a small initial investment towards an asset which buys the firm the right to make future investments to secure that asset.
b. The asset payoff profile is convex; that is, the downside is limited while the potential payoff is very high.
c. The firm has the flexibility to not make any further investments towards the asset and the cost is limited to the initial investment.

If a diversification strategy has the above three attributes, then it is aligned with the real option approach. Oil companies secure exploration rights by paying a relatively small amount to national governments. The payoff profile is convex, as each prospective oil rig/field can generate very high return. The oil companies have the flexibility to not make further investments if their subsequent exploratory activities show that oil is not likely to be found at a particular location.

Real options approach and the four Rs

How do Resources, Recombination, Reach and Roots relate to the real options approach that we have discussed here? These diverse concepts relate to one another in one fundamental way – they are all about the generation of competitive advantage of firms.

Real options are about trial-and-error, trying different things. The extant literature on real options is burdened with arcane calculations borrowed from the domain of financial options. We have ignored that here because we think the greater value of optionality comes from the particular way of strategic thinking it engenders. The distinctive feature of the real options is that it is about real business situations, real assets. In the financial derivatives market, the history of the investor in financial options is immaterial. The value of the underlying asset is in no way connected to the idiosyncrasies of the investor in financial options. But, when it comes to real options, existing resources and capabilities of the firm become central to the investment decision. **Related diversification** is held to be more profitable than **unrelated diversification** because the former allows effective exploitation of existing resources and capabilities of the firm.[5] Real options require less commitment than a full-fledged diversification of business, but the logic of related diversification is valid here as well. In fact, existing resources and capabilities of the firm are often the source of real options that are 'free' to the organization. 'Free' options are **unrecognized options**, they are there for the organization to take advantage of, but the firm may be oblivious to their existence. A university may have lots of talented academics who can provide consultancy services to corporates, yet the institution may not recognize this as an option and fail to act on it. A company may have foreign born employees who can help it bridge the 'psychic distance' to aid its international expansion. It is an option that the firm may or may not recognize.

Real options generate help to recombine ideas and generate innovations. Amazon encourages experimentation with its 'two-way door' system, the two-way door symbolizing the reversibility of a decision. Below is an excerpt from Jeff Bezos's letter to shareholders in 1997:[6]

Invention Machine

We want to be a large company that's also an invention machine. We want to combine the extraordinary customer-serving capabilities that are enabled by size with the speed of movement, nimbleness, and risk-acceptance mentality normally associated with entrepreneurial start-ups.

Can we do it? I'm optimistic. We have a good start on it, and I think our culture puts us in a position to achieve the goal. But I don't think it'll be easy. There are some subtle traps that even high-performing large organizations can fall into as a matter of course, and we'll have to learn as an institution how to guard against them. One common pitfall for large organizations – one that hurts speed and inventiveness – is 'one-size-fits-all' decision making.

Some decisions are consequential and irreversible or nearly irreversible – one-way doors – and these decisions must be made methodically, carefully, slowly, with great deliberation and consultation. If you walk through and don't like what you see on the other side, you can't get back to where you were before. We can call these Type 1 decisions. But most decisions aren't like that – they are changeable, reversible – they're two-way doors. If you've made a suboptimal Type 2 decision, you don't have to live with the consequences for that long. You can reopen the door and go back through. Type 2 decisions can and should be made quickly by high judgment individuals or small groups.

As organizations get larger, there seems to be a tendency to use the heavy-weight Type 1 decision-making *process* on most decisions, including many Type 2 decisions. The end result of this is slowness, unthoughtful risk aversion, failure to experiment sufficiently, and consequently diminished invention. We'll have to figure out how to fight that tendency.

And one-size-fits-all thinking will turn out to be only one of the pitfalls. We'll work hard to avoid it… and any other large organization maladies we can identify.

Amazon's 'two-way-door/type 2' decisions are actually real options, although they do not label them as such. 3M's CEO calls their trial-and-error approach to product innovations 'experimental doodling'.[7] Again, this reflects the real option approach to strategy making. The point we are making here is that there are already some companies who make strategic decisions in a way that parallels the option thinking being described here. We are saying, however, that this way of thinking can benefit even more corporates out there and that it is particularly useful in the current disruptive environment.

Creating options

As mentioned before, the existing literature on real options is preoccupied with discounted cash flow calculations, missing the wood for the trees. The intuitive and experimental approach that we are advocating here has little in common with the conventional strategic thinking on real options. However, Scenario Planning (sometimes referred to as Scenario Thinking or just Scenarios) provides a way to operationalize the idea of real options in real business setting.

Scenarios

Step 1: The focal issue

The first step of formulating a scenario asks the question: what might potentially affect an organization's future the most? Hence, formulating a focal issue of scenario-based planning requires us to also outline the respective decision an organization is expected to make.

The combination of focus and decision is sometimes mentioned as an either/or question. Either a focal issue, or an organizational decision forms the first step to many scenario-building protocols. However, we would argue that combining both elements explicitly offers a far greater benefit to an organization than selecting only a single element. An organizational focal issue appears inseparable from virtually all managerial or organizational decisions to be made.

Step 2: Factors

After an organization's focal issue is defined, the respective factors or elements that might potentially affect an organization are developed. As such, the process of elaborating a range of factors comprises two dimensions.

First, potential areas comprise the internal factors within an organization, such as strategic positioning, customer base, resource constraints and organizational structures. Internal factors are genuinely relatively easy to compile, yet difficult to evaluate when using the established set of organizational routines. For example, a well-established production-chain covering multiple countries can provide strategic benefits to a company. However, those factors or production elements are assessed by means of an established understanding of how an organization is historically used to operate. Shifts in consumer preferences, global imbalances or political factors might influence those production elements and might require an organization to quickly adopt new ways of operating. Defining a set of inter-organizational factors might already require an awareness of those hidden assumptions in defining internal factors.

Second, external factors are defined. These elements are situated in an organization's contextual environment and as such are generally more demanding to identify and to address. However, most organizations are reasonably aware of external factors that have the potential to influence their prospective position. External factors might potentially relate to the entrance of new competitors in an existing market segment or technological substitutes that render a current proposition obsolete in the future. External factors are, for obvious reasons, outside the immediate influence of an organization. As such, an assessment of external factors is mostly reduced to an occasional strategy session by key personnel in an attempt to formulate effective responses. In the context of formulating a scenario, however, the scope and magnitude of external factors is pivotal in developing future scenarios that actually provide organizations with sensible capabilities to cope with those future changes.

Step 3: Forces

Besides the more static view on internal and external factors of scenarios, it is the temporal change of those factors that becomes relevant. As such, it is important to account for the factor of time, trends and shifts in developments. In most instances, the pace of ongoing developments does not necessarily require us to formulate scenarios to come up with a suitable response. Nor is the development itself perceived as a challenge – hence the sheer speed at which a development is unfolding might make many an organization shudder. Slow trends and changes in consumer preferences or the supply of natural resources allow companies to adapt to those changes. It is at the intersection of internal and external factors, and in particular where those factors misalign, where the development of future scenarios yields the biggest strategic insights.

One key element that is generally provided as an example of a force majeure is a geopolitical conflict – war. Extraordinary events or circumstances are not rare in themselves but are generally excluded from more regular business planning tasks as being too remote and unquantifiable. As such, geopolitical developments, environmental challenges and climate changes and, obviously, the outbreak of unexpected pandemics can form a major component of scenario plans, yet those are mostly excluded from regular business activities.

Step 4: Importance and uncertainties

In its fourth step, the process of scenario planning requires us to prioritize among both the number and the magnitude of factors and forces identified so far. In brief, it's about choosing which 'future' is worth developing into a scenario. Thereby, the elements formulated during steps one to three are converted into a condensed set of priorities and uncertainties.

This process of conversion is practically done through a number of voting-ballots by the members of the scenario planning team involved. During this step, the members of the team allocate their votes to the respective focal issue and assign varying degrees of uncertainty to each element. This is easier said than done, and assessing uncertainty of highly unlikely and improbable events is not the strongest element in developing a scenario plan. However, the act of assigning both relevance and degrees of uncertainty to potential forces allows the practitioners to reduce the scope of initial forces and their effects on the organization to a manageable amount. Therefore, step 4 can best be understood as an exercise in professional judgement to propose an informed guess. Hence, please bear in mind that the development of a future scenario is a structured approach to develop capabilities through a process of iterations or organizational learning steps. Therefore, it is not the scenario plan that deserves the most attention but developing the capabilities of organizational learning might best be seen as the purpose of this process.

Step 5: Logics

Deciding between the various 'futures' emerging through step 5 requires us to make some careful considerations about the underlying logics that we apply. It does not make a difference if we call it a genuine ability to assess the logic of our decision making, the ability to review our professional judgement or our ability to learn. What these terms share, is the need to make it explicit which sensible choice among a myriad of 'futures' is potentially affecting our organization. And this sensible choice is hugely affected by historical assumptions, preferences and inertia. Hence, to doubt some of those assumptions and question the underlying preferences is a pivotal capability in developing scenarios.

There is an interesting YouTube channel, reviewing blockbuster movies for logical inconsistencies, called 'Everything wrong with ...'. It illustrates how major movie productions easily run into double-digit flaws of logical inconsistencies, mistakes or examples of just plain nonsense. Therefore, it might help to perform a careful exercise of this game with your own organizational logics when deciding between the various 'futures' to develop. In the end, it is rather challenging to answer what that 'Everything wrong with, ... your way of thinking' entails, but it can provide some valuable insights to your organizational logics.

As such, it helps to draw out a two-dimensional matrix, in which the two most relevant uncertainties are used as axes to the model. For simplicity reasons, this model is used to separate the 'futures' into four categories. Within each quadrant (a) to (d), one scenario to plan for is developed (see Figure 7.2).

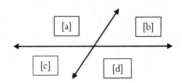

FIGURE 7.2 Scenario planning Step 5: Logics a, b, c and d

In the end, the almost infinite number of 'futures' is reduced to a set of no more than two to three cases, that are worthwhile to develop into scenarios.

Step 6: Scenarios

Up to step 5, we followed a reasonably structured path of activities. In step 6, the number of 'futures' that we identified throughout the previous steps are put into a coherent story. A story that is logically consistent with our focal issue(s), the various factors and forces affecting them, and our relevance and logics applied. Due to the fact that planning for scenarios is by definition an exercise performed by various team members of an organization, the act of writing a coherent story is therefore frequently mentioned as an act of co-creation; or better, as an art of co-creation.

Practically, it helps to split step 6 into two to three sessions of group discussions and workshops to compile the single elements of the scenario-story and perform the actual writing of the scenario in a smaller group of participants. As always, the act of formulating the future-story is almost as important as the individual elements of the story. Content and storytelling have to be put into balance to become a persuasive narrative that actually provides strategic insights to an organization.

As such, the process of writing out a consistent narrative containing all relevant elements, can easily take weeks to several months before completion. Again, we would like to emphasize that we don't see the actual output of the scenario as the single most important purpose of scenario planning, but rather the development of an organizational capability through a set of routines to learn, adapt and strategize.

Step 7: Indicators

Indicators are there to observe, if and when a scenario starts to unfold. The use of early indicators – the canaries in organizational strategy – varies between the different scenarios. Some indicators can best be seen as changes in the behaviour of forward-seeking customers, in some cases it can be a technological development pointing in a certain direction, in yet more cases it is what newspaper headlines begin to publish about various topics.

Early indicators are generally the very first impression of a future change unfolding. However, to correctly observe an indicator as being a relevant part of a future scenario is a pivotal task to formulate a strategic response. As such, being able to correctly identify a relevant indicator and connect it with the range of future scenarios is again an organizational capacity that can best be seen as an iterative skill. Therefore, it is one thing to correctly identify early indicators of emerging trends through your general observation of the environment. It is something completely different though to formulate an adequate strategic response to this indicator.

As such, one single indicator would normally not do all the work required. Identifying early indicators can therefore in itself be seen as an act of carefully monitoring trends and developments and discussing those with members of your organization. We already pointed out that the development of scenarios can best be seen as an act, or better an art of co-creation. Defining and monitoring early indicators can therefore best be considered as putting this art into practice within a specific organizational setting.

Step 8: Evaluate options

In the final step, the move from scenario to strategy is performed. This move requires the members of an organization to formulate a practical response to the unfolding changes the early indicators identified.

The scenario options can be evaluated through the optionality prism. Bounded rationality, which we discussed earlier in the chapter, can be exercised here to focus on scenario options that have convex payoffs as they portend superior profits.

To formulate such a strategic response can be done through a re-assessment of a strategy that is already established. As such, a scenario can be seen as a hypothetical litmus test to examine the position of a current strategy under changing conditions.

A second way to formulate a strategic response is by placing the strategy itself under the hypothetical microscope and review its adaptability to various scenarios. The more versatile a strategy is to adjust to various scenarios, the more suitable it probably is to cope with actual future changes.

Again, to plan for various scenarios is in itself not a process that should be seen as one-stop effort. Scenario planning is a way of structuring a thinking and learning process within an organization. A thinking process to develop new organizational capabilities through multiple iterative steps. And again, the purpose of a scenario plan can better be seen as an act of communicating learning efforts throughout an organization, instead of providing a conclusive view on the future.

This view on communicating learning efforts as an ongoing conversation is brought forward by Kees van der Heijden, who worked on the development of the Shell Global Scenarios.[8] He summarizes the art of co-creating scenarios in the following words:

> If there is one single element essential to success it is being able to develop new and unique insights about the world. Without this no strategy can succeed. An original invention does not come easy, it needs a lot of time, discussion and contemplation. The strategic conversation in the organisation is the basis of its ability to gain such original insights.
>
> *(Van der Heijden, 2011: 346)*

Essentially, the future is not predictable, nor is anybody able to reliably forecast the relevance of changes in the foreseeable future. The strength of scenario planning is formed by providing members of an organization with a tool-box to formulate a narrative of the many possible futures, a tool-box that might potentially help an organization to ultimately find out which tools to apply; as such, it is an act of structured art.

CASE STUDY 7.1: BUSINESS CASE – 3M

When in 1902, the Minnesota Mining and Manufacturing Company, also called MMM, was established by five businessmen, the company's aim was to mine corundum, an aluminium oxide. However, after initial efforts, the company realized that its mineral holdings had no economic value.

Within the first three years of its incorporation, the company's production changed towards a barely related venture. The Minnesota Mining and Manufacturing Company moved from an explorative mining venture into the field of research and production of sandpaper. One and a half decades after that change was made, the company became financially viable and profit-making.

Nowadays, the company is better known by its acronym 3M.[1] The company however still holds to its historic ticker symbol, MMM, at the New York Stock Exchange. Using the same ticker symbol is hardly surprising given the fact that sandpaper is still one of the many products the company produces. And to nobody's surprise, the company's headquarters is in St Paul, Minnesota.

What did change during the last century is the size of the company. As per year end 2019, 3M's market capitalization, or market value of its outstanding stock amounted to US$101.79 billion. As such, the ability to cope with unforeseen changes in the business and to respond in the venture's strategy to new insights played out well for 3M.

And the company's products can be found in almost every single household across the globe.[2] For the company's home-market in the US alone, its product range comprises a staggering 23,911 items in the company's online catalogue according to the company's website in April 2020. Covering a huge area of products such as contact cleaners and still indeed, sandpaper, some of the individual brand names are better known to the general audience than the holding company's name. Most customers across the globe are familiar with products such as Post-it notes, Scotch adhesive tapes and Filtrete filter technology.

However, the general market opinion on companies that are broadly diversified is not always indiscriminate. Listed companies that form a business group across multiple sectors are genuinely penalized by a conglomerate discount. The general perception exists that diversification can better be achieved through a portfolio of stocks held instead of investing in business groups with diversified operations. As such, the remarkable success of 3M showed evidence that conglomerates provide a sensible model to companies.

During the aftermath of the financial crisis of 2007–09, it appeared that 3M was able to utilize internal resources where more focused companies fell short of obtaining cash funds from the market. As Reuters, an international news organization, published in 2012:[3]

Large, multinational conglomerates considering a crash diet may want to think twice if they wish to reward shareholders: the argument that smaller is better is a little less persuasive these days.

The press report continues – citing an analysis from Boston Consulting Group; a strategy consulting firm – and outlines that the widely shared perception among market analysists might at least for US companies have shifted towards a more balanced view on how conglomerates perform.

Yet big conglomerates are regaining favor, as some researchers and long-term shareholders argue that the case for diversification is stronger after the 2007–2009 crisis.

The report concludes that even if the market outperformance of the time under research was only limited (a 6.1% shareholder return for diversified companies compared with 5.8% for more narrowly focused firms), the outperformance was in part achieved with less volatility.

Company structure and results

Currently, the portfolio of business activities of the research-minded company group is organized around the following four business segments. Together, they achieve the company's global net sales of US$32.1 billion.

First, the area of Safety and Industrial comprises personal protection equipment for people working in a wide range of manufacturing, mining or oil and gas companies, as well as medical services or pharmaceutical production. For the United States alone, safety glasses, ear protection and gloves provided US$2.8 billion in sales during 2019, and achieved an operating income of US$586 million. Worldwide, the annual revenue is about US$11.6 billion.

Second, Transportation and Electronics comprises a product portfolio catering to the specific needs of original equipment manufacturers in the automotive and aerospace industry as well as electronic display products. For the US market, the company achieved US$2.3 billion net sales and US$475 million operating income for the year 2019. On a global level, the net sales for the year amounted to US$9.6 billion.

Third, the business segment Health Care reported net sales for the year 2019 for the US market of US$2.1 billion and an operating income of US$457 million. On a global level, the company achieved net sales during the year within this segment, amounting to US$7.4 billion. Products that form part of this area comprise a broad range of medical and surgical supplies.

Fourth and last, the business segment Consumer reports US$1.3 billion sales and an operating income amounting to US$296 million for the year 2019. This segment provides products for home improvement, stationery and office supplies as well as consumer health care. It's within this company unit where the legacy of sandpaper, Post-it notes and Scotch adhesive tapes can be found. The global net sales for this business segment amounted to US$5 billion.

All four business divisions have in common that they share an operating margin varying between 20.9 and 23.4%. The operating income margin over the year 2019 decreased to 19.2% (from 22.0% relative to the prior year's results).

When announcing the company's financial results for the year 2019, 3M's chairman and chief executive officer, Mike Roman, expressed a sound understanding of the company's history to develop new areas of business:[4]

> We also continue to build for the future, including the launch of our new global operating model which represents the next phase of our transformation journey. As a result of our actions, we are well positioned to improve our performance, return to growth and deliver a successful 2020.

The portfolio of 3M displays a number of established products. Hence the company's legacy in sandpaper and household stationery items show a product core that lasts for several decades. However, changes in an extensive range of operational processes and research-intensive products illustrate that while a product like sandpaper remains the same, it is hardly identical to the product from a century ago.

The company's sustainable position is based on research and development. As such, 3M outlines a number of areas in its portfolio that are subject to rigorous changes in the nearer future.

The company portfolio

The Annual Report 2019 of 3M is illustratively titled 'Transforming for the Future'.

The report outlines where the company sees areas to further enhance its portfolio of ventures and operational fields.[5]

While external consulting firms like Boston Consulting Group identified the financial performance of a diversified conglomerate as more profitable and less volatile, 3M concludes in the company's Annual Report 2019, that it succeeded to reduce its scope of businesses since 2012:

> The ongoing review and reshaping of 3M's portfolio is key to maximizing value across our company. Since 2012 we have moved from 40 businesses to 23, while completing more than ten divestitures and 14 acquisitions. In 2019 we continued to actively manage our portfolio, with particular progress in strengthening our health care business.

The decision to enhance its health care segments shows the company's responsiveness and awareness of global macro-trends. 3M is a solidly established brand of personal protection and hygiene equipment in the pharmaceutical production or health industry. For obvious reasons, the company sees changes in demographics, increasing urbanization and global flows of production as desirable tendencies to anticipate. 3M's current portfolio, which shows evidence of a sensible responsiveness to historic trends, illustrates one ability the company possesses which forms the foundation to cope with future trends.

Historically, 3M saw itself as a research-driven company. Hence, the ability to innovate is emphasized by Mike Roman in what might be seen as a vital element in the company's strategy to bridge the past and future of the company:

> Innovation differentiates 3M in the marketplace, and supports organic growth and our long track record of delivering premium margins and return on invested capital. In 2019 we invested $3.6 billion in the combination of research and development and cap-ex, which enables us to both invent and manufacture new and unique solutions for customers.

A production company like 3M relies strongly on a foundation of institutionalized engineering skills and operational expertise to develop and produce both reliable and innovative products. These foundational skills bolster the company's position in the global market place.

3M therefore does not intend to limit itself to specific domains of research and development. To potential new hires, the company's career website illustrates the broad range of technical areas the company engages with:[6]

> With more than 45 core technologies – and growing – we're at the forefront of innovation in nearly every industry you can imagine. In Research & Development, you'll be part of a constant flow of new ideas, making your mark on a product pipeline that improves the lives of millions.

Technical knowledge and the ability to utilize innovation are illustrative, yet somewhat unrefined, examples of the company's business strategy. Interestingly enough however, is the remarkable fact that the company sees support for a business strategy that aims to further intensify its current range of product and industry offerings, business segments and technological capabilities.

As said, conglomerates are genuinely not uncontested by business and investment analysts, and a story to pursue a diversification strategy, both across products and over time, has to be told in an engaging way. This is where the company's self-coined transformation journey comes into play.

The transformation journey

On 28 January 2020 3M issued a press release at the same time as its fourth quarter financial results were published, entailing the future prospects of the company. The report is titled, '3M Accelerates Pace of Transformation Journey'.[7] As the report emphasizes, 'Transformation – along with Portfolio, Innovation and People & Culture' is one of 3M's 'strategic priorities to drive long-term growth and value creation'. One might even want to add that the company's survival and prosperity over more than a century is based on its ability to transform its operations and business portfolio.

The company's journey consists of two elements. First, the development of a new global operating model, comprising five elements to enhance the company's global competitive position, and, second, a more simplified firm structure. The earlier successes with the integration of the four business segments supported the company's belief to further align its four segments with 3M's customers and go-to-market models.

The new business model aims to achieve several benefits to the company's customers and stakeholders. First, some of the ongoing changes that 3M is going to accelerate relate to a higher level of decentralized accountability of individual business groups (i.e. business segments). Second, more attention is going to be spent on the relationship with customers to innovate the company's current product range. A third change that is going to take place also relates to decentralization and aims to increase the speed and effectiveness in decision making processes and customer service. A fourth element comprises simplified reporting lines, and the last area to enhance relates to the utilization of the diverse and vast knowledge base of the company. A knowledge base spread across multiple business segments provides a vital source to adhere the company's capabilities and areas of expertise.

The second element in 3M's journey consists of a leaner and more simplified firm structure.

Mike Roman explains this vision for the nearer future in his own words:

> 3M continues to transform how it operates and build a more customer-driven and streamlined organization for the future. The last phase of our transformation journey is designed to improve growth and operational efficiency, and will enable us to create even more value for our customers and shareholders. This is a defining moment in how we run our company, and positions 3M for success in the years ahead.

3M identifies three areas that are elementary to enhance efficiency across the various functional entities. The firm had already restructured a number of production areas but aims to further enhance its operations through consolidation across the full scope of the company's functional areas, 'manufacturing, supply chain and customer operations'. Those areas were intended to be unified into a single Enterprise Operations unit with the prime focus to create a 'customer experience end-to-end'.

A second domain comprises a new organizational unit – Corporate Affairs. This business unit acquired the responsibility to advance and protect brand value and reputation of 3M on a global level. Third, all currently existing corporate support functions will be realigned to further enhance the effectiveness of the company across both geographies and operational areas.

The company explained how it achieved its current position. Which operational steps are going to be taken is also clearly outlined. What remains to assess is the company's view on which abilities the enterprise requires to be able to adjust to future changes. This is where 3M's Sustainability Report can help to enhance our understanding of one of 3M's vital business skills.

'Outside-the-box-thinking' in 3M's 2019 Sustainability Report

Besides the two areas of personal protection equipment and cleaning products, 3M's 2019 sustainability report describes how the company views its strategic options for the future,[8] how those are developed, assessed and put to work. Titled, 'Improving every life', the company's report explains what it means to be a 'purpose-driven enterprise'. Cassandra Garber, 3M Global Sustainability Leader, emphasizes the role of science in organizing the firm's operations, as follows:

> Because 3M is a science-based company with diverse operations and a large product portfolio serving nearly every industry across the globe, we're in a unique position to make impact ourselves, and enable impact by others. Our new Strategic Sustainability Framework demonstrates where our critical opportunity as a company meets the critical opportunity of our world and gives us a means of prioritizing how to most effectively take action.

The role of science and scientific reasoning is a much-acknowledged element in the company's strategy. It appears that this factor is engrained in the *raison d'être* of 3M. Without scientific methods, the company would not have been what it is nowadays. The very first move from a mining-venture into a sandpaper production firm was based on structured insights grounded in a scientific approach to its product development.

It's the company's capability to assess various hypothetical alternatives scientifically that drives 3M's firm strategy as the Sustainability Report 2019 continues to outline:

> Science operates within a set of rules. It follows specific methods. It delivers proof and proves cause and effect. But science also breaks boundaries, challenges the status quo, and improves lives.

As a company rooted in scientific exploration and the belief that every problem has a solution, we are applying our technological expertise to help solve some of the world's biggest challenges. The challenges we must tackle for a sustainable future don't always follow clear rules or methods – but we see them clearly. They are broad. They are interrelated. They are solvable. We know science can help tackle them.

3M illustrates how its historic experience is translated into a contemporary set of company skills to respond to broad and interrelated yet solvable challenges. As such, the company does incorporate many a learning aspect that time has brought to the repository of the company. To translate those lessons into scientific knowledge that is solid enough to remain relevant is pivotal for the company's success. The art of organizing a conglomerate across multiple business segments and yet keeping sandpaper on the company's production chain illustrates how more than a single product and more than a single technical skill might form an award-winning and clearly remarkable combination.

Pointers to strategic conversation

1. How different is 3M's strategy-making compared to other players in the market?
2. What benefits accrue to 3M through its trial and error approach to product development?
3. What are the main downsides of the trial and error approach to strategy-making?

Sources

[1] 3M, official company website: www.3m.com
[2] 3M, official company website, Product Catalog US: www.3m.com/3M/en_US/company-us/all-3m-products/~/All-3M-Products/?N=5002385+8711017+3294857497&rt=r3
[3] Reuters – Diversified companies shrink 'conglomerate discount', 27 February 2012: www.reuters.com/article/us-conglomerates/diversified-companies-shrink-conglomerate-discount-idUSTRE81Q1R420120227
[4] 3M, official company website, 3M News Center – Q4 and full-year 2019 results: https://news.3m.com/press-release/company-english/3m-reports-fourth-quarter-and-full-year-2019-results-implements-new-gl
[5] 3M Annual Report 2019 – Transforming for the future: https://s24.q4cdn.com/834031268/files/doc_financials/2019/ar/2019-3m-annual-report.pdf
[6] 3M, official company website, 3M Careers: www.3m.com/3M/en_US/careers-us/working-at-3m/our-business-groups/

7 3M, official company website, 3M News Center – Press Release: https://
news.3m.com/press-release/company-english/3m-accelerates-pace-
transformation-journey

8 3M, official company website, 3M Sustainability – 2019 Sustainability
Report: www.3m.com/3M/en_US/sustainability-us/annual-report/ And as
pdf-document: https://multimedia.3m.com/mws/media/1691941O/2019-
sustainability-report.pdf

Conclusion

In this chapter, we have diverged from conventional strategic thinking and charted
a different path. Conventional strategic thinking is dominated by the planning paradigm. We have pointed out in this chapter that this approach is much less effective
under conditions of disruptive uncertainty. We have suggested that strategic management studies needs to junk hyper-rationality and embrace option thinking
which emphasizes agility and flexibility.

Notes

1 See Rumelt et al., 1991.
2 For an entertaining exposition of the abstraction that is Homo economicus, see Thaler,
2000.
3 See Simon, 1972.
4 See Taleb, 2012.
5 See Chatterjee and Wernerfelt, 1988, for an empirical investigation. The study found
strong support for the idea that related diversification is a more profitable diversification
strategy.
6 Jeff Bezos articulated his 'reversible decision' (real options in our schema) in Amazon's
SEC filings in 1997. The document is available here: www.sec.gov/Archives/edgar/data/
1018724/000119312516530910/d168744dex991.htm.
7 'Encourage experimental doodling. If you put fences around people, you get sheep. Give
people the room they need'. – Chairman of 3M, cited from *Harvard Business Review* article
that can be found here: https://hbr.org/2013/08/the-innovation-mindset-in-acti-3.
8 See van der Heijden, 2011.

Further reading

Chatterjee, S., & Wernerfelt, B. (1988, August). Related or unrelated diversification: A
resource based approach. In *Academy of management proceedings* (Vol. 1988, No. 1, pp. 7–11).
Briarcliff Manor, NY: Academy of Management.
Rumelt, R. P., Schendel, D., & Teece, D. J. (1991). Strategic management and eco-
nomics. *Strategic management journal, 12*(S2): 5–29.
Simon, H. A. (1972). Theories of bounded rationality. *Decision and organization, 1*(1), 161–176.
Taleb, N. N. (2012). *Antifragile: Things that gain from disorder* (Vol. 3). New York: Random House.
Taylor, F. W. (1919). *The principles of scientific management*. New York: Harper & brothers.

Thaler, R. H. (2000). From homo economicus to homo sapiens. *Journal of economic perspectives*, *14*(1), 133–141.

Tversky, A., & Kahneman, D. (1974). Judgment under uncertainty: Heuristics and biases. *Science*, *185*(4157), 1124–1131.

Van der Heijden, K. (2011). *Scenarios: The art of strategic conversation*. Chichester: John Wiley & Sons.

8

BRINGING IT ALL TOGETHER

In this concluding chapter we explain why competitive success is almost never monocausal. Competitive advantage of the firm never rests solely on a resource or even a bundle of resources. It is never built purely on the ability to innovate or internationalize operations. A firm cannot just take a free ride on the advantages that its national environment provides. Competitive advantage invariably arises out of a complex mix of interrelated factors.

As we suggested in Chapter 1, the four Rs act as prompters for evaluating firm competitiveness

a. Where are their roots?
b. How far is their reach?
c. What resources can they control, and/or have access to?
d. How good are they at recombining ideas and resources?

Generally speaking, companies get a better shot at competitive success if they have

a. Roots in innovative economies
b. Reach that is extensive, stretching beyond national boundaries
c. Resources that are superior to those of their competitors
d. Recombinatorial capability that allows them to innovate

Make a list of successful firms that are out there. Even without looking at the specifics of that list, we can say that the companies in your list are likely to have, at the minimum, two of the above, if not all four. What you will not find in your list is an example of a firm whose success is based on only one of the four success factors.

Let's see how the four Rs help us in understanding competitive success in a global context. To do this we will revisit some of the cases presented in previous chapters. The case studies were used to illuminate a specific success factor, but we will see here how that factor interacted with the other variables to generate competitive success.

Take the case of IKEA, presented in Chapter 5 (Reach). IKEA's international reach has undoubtedly enhanced its competitive advantage. But IKEA's greater reach is made possible by its innovative product innovations – its flat pack furniture and its unique stores with in-store restaurants serving Swedish meatballs. These innovations are based on IKEA's resources and capabilities, particularly its ability to come up with cool Scandinavian designs. Last but not least, IKEA's success is bound together with specific aspects of its national environment. The national environment ensures a steady supply of skilled designers and highly qualified professionals. The relatively small size of the national economy also motivated IKEA to go overseas, extending its reach to access new markets and factors of production. You can see here that IKEA's competitive success is a product of distinct yet interrelated factors. It is possible though to construct a hierarchy of the causal factors. One can argue that IKEA's resources and capabilities have played a more salient role in its competitive success than the other three Rs.

Consider the case of Netflix which features in Chapter 4 (Recombination). Netflix has excelled in recombinatorial activities, innovating in terms of both the delivery and content of media entertainment. To do this effectively, Netflix's internal resources and capabilities were vital, but the sources of these organizational assets were linked to their roots in Silicon Valley. The state of California in the United States hosts both Silicon Valley and Hollywood. These facts are not coincidental in relation to Netflix's competitive success. To a large extent, Netflix's competitive advantage is built on these geographical advantages. As a startup Netflix benefited from the availability of venture capital in the Silicon Valley region, and when it entered its growth phase, it took advantage of the TV and movie production capabilities of California to come up with Netflix original content.

In Chapter 5, Apple's global reach has been highlighted as one of its key success factors. Apple's reach has allowed its core resources (the company's portfolio of products) to be exploited effectively. Extending one's reach brings access to new markets and factors of production. But Apple's roots in Silicon Valley contributed to the development of its resources and capabilities. Steve Jobs, Apple's talismanic CEO for a long time, was a local lad who grew up in the region.

We see from the above, that competitive success is rarely monocausal. The different factors are interrelated in interesting ways. Take 'Resources' and 'Recombination' for example. Recombination is about innovation which can be in the form of product and process. Product innovations like Apple's iPad are built on specific organizational resources and capabilities. Referring to Porter's Generic Strategies, we can see the link between the differentiation strategy and product innovation, and between the cost leadership strategy and process innovation. We have seen that extending a firm's reach gains access to new markets and factors of production, but internationalization is dependent on organizational specific assets, which are in turn often impacted by the home environment (Roots, Chapter 6) of the company.

FIGURE 8.1 The four Rs of competitive success (restatement of Figure 1.1)

We are not saying that all four Rs – Resources, Recombination, Roots and Reach – will be equally important in all instances. The mix will be invariably different from case to case. In a specific case, resources and roots may matter more than recombination and reach. In another, the causal mix would be different. The four Rs of competitive success is a conceptual framework, it alerts you to the possible factors of success; the model aids the start of a strategic conversation.

How does the idea of optionality, which we discussed in Chapter 7, fit in with the four Rs of competitive success? Optionality works best when the external environment is fraught with uncertainty, which makes long-term strategic planning a very difficult proposition. In Chapter 2, we discussed the two main drivers of uncertainty: globalization and digitization. When global flows of goods, services, capital and ideas circulate in high velocity within a nation, the macro environment becomes unpredictable. Optionality is about recognizing that uncertainty is Janus-faced, it portends both risks and opportunities. Optionality is about convexity in payoffs – keeping the downside small and the upside open. In Chapter 7 we discussed the case of 3M. The company experiments with many different product lines, and is comfortable with failures. It expects many of the product lines to fail but is confident that a few will become popular with the consumers and generate superior returns that will recoup all the losses of failed products and provide a profit for the firm. Option thinking is essentially about embracing uncertainty.

Optionality is linked to diversification and consequently it can be thought of as part of corporate strategy. Optionality is not so much about explaining competitive success of the past, it is more about navigating the choppy waters and managing to stay afloat in the foreseeable future. The four Rs affect optionality in interesting ways. Existing resources and capabilities of the firm sometimes represent 'free' options. The potential of these resources to generate a different revenue stream for the firm has not yet been recognized, but the possibility is there. These 'free' options can be in the form of possible new products and/or services, and access to new overseas markets. The national environment can also provide free options to the firm: for example, the ability to use the 'made in Germany' label opens up interesting possibilities for German firms. Of course, many real options are not free, and companies have to make additional investments to secure them, but even in such cases, there are often synergies between the underlying assets of these options and existing resources and capabilities of the firm.

In Chapter 7 (Creating options) we have explored the link between entrepreneurialism and option thinking. We have suggested that entrepreneurs are generally good at spotting business opportunities with convex payoffs. Some entrepreneurial firms like 3M embrace uncertainty wholeheartedly and experiment with multiple business opportunities (bearing convex payoffs) simultaneously, manifesting the trial-and-error approach which lies at the heart of option thinking. Companies can profit from option thinking when the macro-environment becomes disruptively uncertain, a situation that makes conventional management tools less useful as guides for strategic action.

The theories and frameworks covered in this book should not be taken as physical laws that are applicable universally. The ideas, concepts and frameworks included in this book are more like heuristics, rules of the thumb – in many cases they can illuminate and/or be a guide to strategic action, in some instances they may not be particularly relevant. That is the nature of the beast.

Strategy is about competitive success. Strategy is not about managers making clever, abstract plans that are divorced from the reality of their day to day business. Strategic intelligence within the firm is not organized hierarchically even though the organization itself can be hierarchical. A person at the bottom of the hierarchy can have more strategic insight to the business than someone who is at the top. It is important to harvest the strategic intelligence that lies dispersed across the firm and the prompters are there to aid the start of strategic conversations within the organization.

If you are a student, teacher or researcher of strategy, the above prompters can aid your analysis of a firm's competitive success. You should regard the theories and frameworks as tools in your toolkit for strategy making. Not all ideas will be relevant all the time, there is necessarily an element of choice. Choosing the right framework, tool or method for the job is a skill by itself.

In conclusion, this book has equipped you with ideas, concepts and frameworks that not only help you to analyse and understand organizational competitive success attained in the past but some of them also aid strategic decision making which is necessarily oriented towards the future.

INDEX

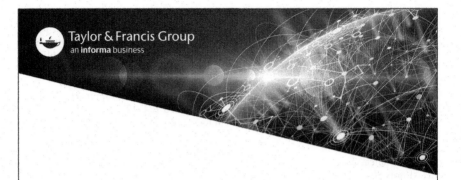